MW01520967

Business Fables & Foibles

By

Ron Moore

Copyright 2013

Other Books by Ron Moore

Making Common Sense Common Practice:
Models for Operational Excellence
(From MRO-Zone.com & Amazon.com)

What Tool? When?
A Management Guide for Selecting the Right Improvement Tools
(From MRO-Zone.com & Amazon.com)

Our Transplant Journey:
A Caregiver's Story
(From Amazon.com)

The RM Group, Inc.
12024 Broadwood Drive
Knoxville, TN 37934, USA

Copyright © 2013, The RM Group, Inc. All rights reserved.

No part of this publication may be reproduced, stored in a retrieval system, or transmitted in any form or by any means, electronic, mechanical, photocopying, recording, or otherwise without the prior written permission of the publisher.

Permission may be sought directly from The RM Group, Inc., Phone: 1-865-675-7647.

ISBN-13: 978-1482055924
ISBN-10: 1482055929

Cover by Todd Schott, Knoxville, TN

This book is dedicated to all those who strive daily within their business to make it successful,
in spite of poor management.

Table of Contents

Preface

This book began when I became frustrated while attempting to write an op-ed piece to submit to a major newspaper. The topic was layoffs and how they can destroy value in an organization. I had drafted the piece and sent it to a friend of mine who worked for the paper, looking for his feedback before submitting it.

His reply began with "I hope we're still friends after you read my review." We were. I wasn't offended by his review and suggestions – too wordy, not succinct enough, better focus here, etc., along with the usual editorial corrections. This was my first pass at something like this, so I thought his comments were very constructive. I took another pass at it and sent it to him again. Better, he said, but the implication was that it was still pretty ordinary. He offered a few additional suggestions. I took a third pass at it, and not wanting to bother him again, sent the piece to the paper. I never heard from them, and having a sense for the obvious, assumed it had been rejected.

In an effort to work out my frustration with trying to articulate an important message, I wrote a light-hearted satirical, fictitious story to convey that message. I sent this to him, and his response was "I love it!" My conclusion was that my talent, as limited as it is, did not lie in writing op-ed pieces, but would be better applied to writing short, whimsical, satirical stories. Thus began a series of stories, the sum of which make up this book, and my effort to characterize the foibles of many businesses. While the purist might more accurately describe these stories as parables, I've chosen the alliterative phrase of 'fables and foibles'. I hope you will indulge my shortcoming in this inaccuracy.

The stories are mostly based on my experience in working with manufacturing companies, and all the pressures that relate to their efforts to be competitive, and particularly the extreme pressures for lower costs.

Why is there such pressure? My answer is simple. For a given set of requirements in an item that we're going to buy, almost all of us tend to *buy the cheapest item that meets our requirements*. This puts pressure on prices, which in turn puts pressure on costs. So, it's not surprising that when manufacturers perceive they can make a product cheaper elsewhere, no matter where that is, they will go there, so they can be more competitive. To remain competitive also demands that our productivity improve year on year. Managers seem to understand these basic principles, but many fail to understand that lower costs are achieved through engaging the workforce in improving the processes, as opposed to simple cost cutting. It's also surprising how many employees don't understand these simple principles, and seek higher wages and benefits without commensurate improvements in productivity, thus putting their jobs at risk. They too tend to buy the cheapest item that meets their requirements.

The stories cover numerous topics, but there is a set of recurring themes, so I hope you'll forgive a certain amount of repetitiveness in the lessons from the stories.

In his landmark, but boringly titled book, Organizational Psychology, Edgar Schein observed that the process of organizing creates naturally competing groups – individuals, departments, shifts, areas, plants, divisions, etc. That is, people are naturally competitive, and often want "bragging rights". His observations and conclusions were well researched and have several experimental studies to confirm them.

Among other things, he states that *alignment is critical where task **inter**-dependence makes collaboration essential for organizational effectiveness.* In every organization there is a huge amount of task inter-dependence, for example, between marketing and manufacturing, between purchasing and operations, between accounting and purchasing, between production and maintenance, between shifts in a manufacturing plant, and so on. The list goes on.

Put simply, when we depend on one another to get a job done, we must work together toward a common purpose or objective to be more effective. Said differently, when were focus only on our goals without consideration of other departments, we are not likely to be as successful as an organization. The greater good, or the good of all, should be given a higher priority. According to Schein, overcoming this tendency to compete, rather than work together, requires the creation of *superordinate*, or higher level, goals that take priority over "group" interests, and that align us to that purpose.

And this is where most companies do a poor job. Indeed, many companies encourage *destructive competition*, to the overall detriment of company performance.

To counter this tendency toward destructive competition, it is essential that the leadership articulate the higher level goals and constantly remind people to focus on these, and that they encourage people to work together toward a common purpose, to think at a systems level, rather than optimizing at the suboptimal level, in their little silo. To support this there is the need to develop shared measures between "competing" groups and partnership agreements, so that the basis for the collaboration and teamwork is clear, and an effective balance is achieved.

Thus, my stories, though each is different, will have this recurring theme of the need to work together toward a higher purpose, and to think at a systems level regarding the overall objectives of the business. And, as noted, my stories will have a manufacturing and heavy industry bias, but the lessons from the stories are likely universal.

As usual, and as Robert Fulghum observed, the truth of parable does not compete with the truth of science or the courtroom, so I've taken wide latitude in applying the lessons from my experience in writing these tales. So, as you might expect, the names, characters, and incidents are fictitious, and represent an amalgam of the hundreds of people I've met and companies I've worked with. Any resemblance to actual people or events is entirely coincidental.

I hope you enjoy the stories, and that their lessons help you improve your business, and life.

Ron Moore
Knoxville, TN

Part I

Of General Interest

Our People Are
Our Most Important Asset?

1

Once upon a time there was a very successful company, one which was the talk of the town, and whose CEO was admired widely as a hard-nosed business man who "delivered" to Wall Street. For several years now his company, DGC, had grown in sales and earnings every single year. The CEO's nickname was "BL" for he could quickly cut through any silly arguments and get to the bottom line. BL was a very demanding boss, as those bosses tended to be, and yet he always bragged about his employees - "Our employees are our most important asset" he often gushed.

Sad to say, however, BL could see dark clouds looming on the horizon. After years of economic expansion and building a highly respected company, he was seriously concerned about a quickly developing economic downturn. "How can we manage this, something we've never been through before?" he mused. He was using the "*royal we*" of course. It was the first time *he* had seen this, at least in his capacity as CEO. Calling on his friends and board, he pondered this at length. In his head he could hear their voices "Your overhead is too high; your productivity is too low; you've grown so fast you haven't stopped to improve your efficiency; the market is softening, but you've got to hold your margins." and other similar voices.

Panic set in. Sweat broke out. Pulse and blood pressure rose. Now his people seemed lazy, slow, soft, even slovenly. The good times were rolling... right over a cliff. Now, his reputation was at stake, not to mention his ego and stock holdings.

Growing increasingly frustrated, and bowing to these pressures, he finally reached a decision that alas, these people assets were also pretty doggone expensive. They just weren't as productive any more – lazy bums, they'd gotten soft with all the good times. Not much of an asset when you're losing money on all these free loaders. He'd teach them a lesson. He'd have a layoff. That should get their attention, and fatten the company coffers, not to mention salvaging his ego and stock options.

"Wait!" cried Sheila B. Rite, his HR manager (you know, the one with the bleeding heart). "We can't do this! Our marketing manager says the market will come back next year, stronger than ever. And, our new product development manager agrees."

"What do we do in the meantime" responded BL, "These people are costing us a fortune. Where's the payback? We have to hold our budgets."

"But boss, think about how much we've invested in these people- in recruiting, interviewing, re-locating, training, outfitting, and making valued employees. My analysis says it's about $50,000 per employee just to hire them and get them fully productive" wailed Sheila. "Are we going to just write that off?"

"Don't be silly. We don't carry that on our books! We expensed that as it occurred. No one will ever see that" rebutted BL, "You know we only carry fixed capital assets on our books, and we depreciate those."

"But boss, I know we expense the cost of hiring, but it's still an investment, isn't it, just like the money we've invested in all our fixed assets? You wouldn't throw those away would you?

And, what about all the appreciation in the value in our people? Think about all the things they've learned about our products, our customers, our future. Think about all the training we've done with them. Think about all the raises and promotions we've given them. We're paying them for the value they've acquired in their experience aren't we?" Sheila cried out again.

"My analysis says their intellectual capital is worth another $50,000 per employee, and you're going to write it off?" Sheila asked incredulously, "And, suppose marketing and product development are right and the economy does come back, we'll have to re-hire and re-train all those people again, for another $50,000 - $100,000. That doesn't sound too smart. And, laying off people, isn't that an admission of OUR failure, not theirs?" Sheila wasn't known for her political sensitivity.

"Intellectual what? Our failure?" BL responded, face reddening, "That's not on our books either. We won't take a charge on that. What in the world are you going on about? We're paying them way too much for what they're getting done for us. They've just gotten too expensive." He hadn't heard much else either, except for the 'doesn't sound too smart' and 'our failure' dig.

"But, but, but boss" sounding like a broken motor boat at this point and clearly frustrated, Sheila plaintively asked, "Won't the board be upset about these assets being disposed?"

Teeth clinched, BL became really annoyed, "Hell no, the board only cares about how much people cost, not their so-called value, and how that cost will affect the bottom line... this quarter! Now stop bothering me with this nonsense."

Sheila quickly and quietly took her leave, pondering to herself, "What a metamorphosis this has been. Our people have quickly gone from being our most important asset to being our biggest expense, all driven by a downturn in the market. I wonder if BL sees his fixed plant and equipment as expenses or as assets. It's not cheap to keep all that equipment on the books, what with maintenance, insurance, taxes, depreciation, and so on. I wonder if we carried the value of the people on the books like we do the equipment whether he'd feel the same way, if he had to take a big charge on writing off all those human assets.

Alas, the pressure was just too much and what was to be, was to be. BL laid off 10% of the work force.

Bam! Immediately morale took a nosedive, the coffee pot was surrounded by nervous people wondering about their future (and very little work was getting done). Many were putting out their resumes and taking the first job that came along. Lots of political positioning was going on, and maybe even a little back stabbing. Within a month several managers realized that some of the wrong people had been let go, some of which had to be re-hired as contractors, at significantly higher pay. Those who were left behind now had to pick up the slack for those who had left, for you see, while the people had been eliminated, the work they were doing hadn't. But, their heart wasn't in it. Productivity dropped. Boy, this wasn't working so well. The costs hadn't dropped linearly, and the productivity hadn't increased linearly. Au contraire! So much for linear thinking.

Well, time passed as it always does, and things finally settled down, and people got into a groove (or was it a rut?). Lo and behold, at the end of the year, the company had pretty good earnings, but growth was a bit down.

After all, the economy was in a downturn. But now the economy seemed to be growing again, which made BL pretty happy. Now sales would increase. But, he didn't want to hire any more people. After all the past year had been pretty traumatic for him too, what with his ego at stake and all! But, no hiring would be allowed. We needed to be more productive. And, no replacing those disloyal bums that left!

"We've got to run lean and mean" BL exclaimed, "And by the way, we need to take at least 5% out of our costs every year." Of course BL didn't have a clue about how to do that, beyond barking orders. He just knew that people could figure it out.

Sales were pretty flat the following year, but hey, with the cost reductions, earnings were still pretty good. This was working! No more gushing about our employees being our most valuable asset. You had to ride'em hard and demand that they perform.

Being under lots of pressure, BL kept hearing voices, including one in particular, an old Deming adage "Your system is perfectly designed to give you the results that you get;" and "If you remove resource from the system without changing the basic design, system performance will ultimately decline." BL wasn't sure where these voices were coming from, but he was becoming more worried, and ambivalent in his feelings. Sales weren't growing very much, but boy they sure were running lean and mean (or was it skinny and pissed?); and earnings were still doing pretty good weren't they? This was just too subtle for BL.

But what about the improving economy and anticipated increased sales? Well, all the people were hunkered down, getting the things done they knew they had to do, and picking up the slack for those who had left, or were leaving.

There was little time for process improvement, innovation, and new product development. Hunker down, work hard, keep your nose clean, don't be too visible, don't challenge any decisions, be very risk averse.

Hu oh! It was the third year of this new culture at DGC and things didn't feel so good. Yes, the economy had improved, but DGC's sales were still pretty anemic, especially in new products and customers, and the cost reductions hadn't been as good as BL's demands. Well, the budgets had been cut, but the total costs actually incurred weren't getting a lot better, and maybe they'd moved from one category to another. It seems that a lot of work had to be redone, quality had suffered, and customers were getting pretty annoyed.

Cold sweaty palms, hot flashes, nervousness... What was happening? BL's mind was spinning... He continued to hear voices whispering over and over "Your system is perfectly designed to give you the results that you get, and if you remove resource from the system without changing the basic design, system performance will decline." Could this be? Nah! It was those lazy bums who weren't being productive. They were just costing too much. Earnings weren't very good, so we just needed another round of layoffs. That would do it! That would improve the bottom line! But he could still hear the voices whispering. And, he could hear Sheila wailing (she had left under duress long ago, after an act of desperation in rudely challenging BL's "wisdom" in not valuing the employees). "Damn, why are these voices bothering me?" lamented BL.

Another round of layoffs ensued, but this time it didn't work as well, if you can even say that the first round actually worked. Morale took another nosedive, lots of people left, and the customers were wondering just what was going on.

Some customers decided that they'd just had enough. Company performance declined even further. The stock price took a dive.

DGC is now a wisp of its former self. BL retired, and actually did pretty well financially. Being the smart guy that he was, he'd diversified his portfolio right after the first round of layoffs. Except, his ego suffered enormously from his firing.

The Lessons: 1) Your employees really are your most important asset. 2) Equipment depreciates in value; employees appreciate in value. You should account for both. 3) When climbing rapidly, be careful to avoid a stall, and crash.

CEO Pay – How to Demotivate Employees, and Fail

2

Ibyn Ovyrpayd was a highly accomplished executive. He was born in Eastern Europe to poor parents who emigrated to the US in hopes of a better future. And, better it was, for everyone, but particularly for Ibyn. He worked his way through college, and with the help of his parents, scholarships, and work-study programs ultimately received his bachelors and masters degrees. This hard work ethic throughout his career, and a little luck, finally landed him the position of CEO of Ballarat Company. He was now handsomely paid, typically millions each year.

One day, out of the blue, he received the following letter:

> Dear Mr. Ovyrpayd:
>
> The purpose of this letter is to provide you with the benefit of my observations over the past few years with the hope that it will help in your efforts to move the company forward. These observations are blunt, and intended to inform, but not offend. Specifically, my hope is that these will help you understand the negative impact that your compensation is having on the organization, and ultimately, the success of your company. But before continuing, let me introduce myself. I'm Thorn Inyurside, a middle manager, and one of your most loyal and long-time employees. I've served the company for the past 30 years, but will be retiring next week. Before leaving, however, I wanted to share these observations, which are typical of most all my peers and subordinates, and indeed the majority of your employees.

While we think you've done an OK job, perhaps a C+ or B-overall, we don't think that you deserve the millions that have been showered upon you for mediocre performance. Our company's profit over the past several years has been near our industry average, likewise for our return on capital and revenue growth. We have no new "block-buster" products pending, at least that I know of. In fact, we've been concerned for years now about how little we've spent on R&D for new products and processes; on our marketing and distribution systems; and particularly on maintenance in our manufacturing plants. Even more troubling is that these modest profits seem to be only because of the company's short-term cost cutting in these areas, putting the future of the company at risk. Perhaps you'll be gone by the time these effects are realized, but in the meantime you certainly do talk a good game. Your eloquence is mesmerizing, but given the company's performance compared to your pay, it's not clear whether you're dazzling us with brilliance, or baffling us with bullstuff.

Let's be clear. We believe you deserve to be paid handsomely. But, did you know that you've received pay raises of 10-25% per year over the past five years, but us folks doing the work of keeping the company running have received 3-4%. Or, did you know that your pay over the past several years has been some 400 times that of our average hourly employee. That's up from 40 times the average 30 years ago. Imagine – you could have saved 300 jobs by receiving only 100 times that of the average worker.

It feels like we do the work, and you get the money. Somehow that doesn't seem fair, nor does it align our interests with company interests. Quite the contrary. There's just something wrong about this – you are getting a huge payout at the expense of your employees, particularly those who have been laid off. It's demoralizing. Many of us (not me, I'm retiring) spend our time worrying about whether we're next to be laid off, as opposed to looking for ways to help the company do better.

Did you know that we surveyed 50 of my peers last year regarding your pay? To a person, middle managers were resentful of what they considered your excessive pay. While they were committed to their jobs, they were *not* committed to the company, *nor* fully engaged in executing your strategy. It gets even worse when you talk to the union leadership. They're questioning giving up benefits and pay, when you're being rewarded excessively, at their expense; and they're questioning improving productivity, only to see jobs going overseas, or simply going away. Something is wrong when regular payrolls are skinny and your pay is obese. This situation makes your strategy untenable, and puts the company's future at risk, notwithstanding how eloquently you present it.

Now, just so you feel better about all this, your situation is much like most of the Fortune 500 companies. There are numerous studies (I've read several personally) that show there is no correlation between CEO pay and company performance. One study found that over a five year period top executive pay increased by 77%, while earnings growth increased by only 17%. Your pay mirrors this performance. How would you feel if we expected huge annual pay raises for performance like that?

We understand that there are a lot of very intelligent people, including your board of directors, who rationalize your pay with certain arguments. By the way, Merriam-Webster says that to rationalize is *"to attempt to justify behavior normally considered irrational or unacceptable by offering an apparently reasonable explanation."* That describes our observations of your pay, which seems irrational and unacceptable, in spite of the efforts of your board to rationalize it.

One rationale that is often used to justify CEO pay is the sports star analogy. That is, sports stars command huge salaries commensurate with what the market will bear. So, the argument goes, should CEOs.

This argument is faulty. Sports stars don't have thousands working for them, or people who look to them as a role model for leadership, and fairness! Sports stars often focus on their personal success, more so than the team's, and behave in an egomaniacal manner. Is this the model you want to emulate? Is this the model of behavior that will inspire your employees to make the company successful? Hardly. We believe that you have a fiduciary duty to put the needs of the company above your personal needs, and that you must lead by example, one that creates a sense of fairness, alignment, and teamwork within the company. You currently do not.

Another rationale is the competitive parity argument. Unfortunately, all CEO compensation over the past two or three decades has been rising sharply, with each successive CEO chasing ever increasing compensation packages, using peer averages that have been climbing ~10% per year, while corporate profits have grown only modestly. If you listen to Prairie Home Companion, you'll recognize this as the Lake Wobegon effect, where *everyone* is above average. It's a statistical impossibility.

So, what should you do? We think you should use the principle that compensation must be **"internally equitable and externally competitive"** as a basis for developing policies and guidelines for executive pay. This simple principle is discussed below.

Internal equitability has to do with the perception that compensation is fair. If pay isn't perceived as internally equitable, morale and motivation will deteriorate, and affect company performance, as demonstrated by the survey of 50 middle managers. We understand that totally eliminating any sense of inequity is highly unlikely, but having a clear policy that provides a transparent, well communicated approach to compensation will help. You currently do not.

The vast majority of people expect that people of higher rank, authority, or responsibility will be paid more. How much more? W. Edward Deming suggested that once the CEO's compensation goes beyond about 20 times the wage of the average employee that a sense of *in*equity prevails. Warren E. Buffett has called executive pay the acid test of governance, and "…often tells corporate chiefs to end practices ranging from huge CEO pay to incomprehensible financial reports." The higher the gap between CEO pay and the regular worker, the greater the sense of inequity that's likely, reducing morale and productivity. And, the greater the inequity, the more militant unions will be. This inequity is a huge distraction from the success of the company.

As a matter of policy, we believe you and your board of directors should follow the principle of internal equity and external competitiveness, applying the following in setting your compensation:

1. Overall industry performance must be used effectively as a normalizing factor. As the old saying goes, "Everyone's boat rises in a rising tide." Current policy ignores this. If the company's industry shows strong annual growth, return on equity, profits, etc., and the company is performing near the industry's average, then your pay should reflect average performance.

2. Strategic issues, and your pay, should relate to the company's success in 3, 5, and 10 years. Being strategic relates to your ability to understand the consequences of your decisions over the time frame associated with your level of responsibility. Incentivizing you with huge pay packages and stock options that vest in one or two years is *not* being strategic at your level of responsibility.

3. The concept of being strategic also requires fairness. Our annual results have been at the expense of reduced R&D and marketing, layoffs, low pay increases, and longer hours for the people who do the day-to-day work to

make the company successful, and you wealthier. These create a perception of unfairness, or inequity in the compensation system. If executive salaries are seen to reflect greed and abuse of power, an atmosphere is created where lower productivity, tweaking of expenses and other less than honest practices become common. It currently does.

4. Finally, as the lead representative of shareholders, you have an inherent fiduciary duty to lead the company in achieving a high level of performance, *long term*. You should not be paid extravagantly for doing the job you were hired to do. How would you respond to employees demanding significantly higher pay, year on year, for doing what they were hired to do?

In closing, we understand that in a global, capitalistic economy, the intense competition for survival and prosperity dictates that wages be constrained, *including yours*, and that productivity improvement be substantially greater than wage and cost increases to assure continued competitive position. Those situations that lead to a dysfunctional and unsustainable outcome, i.e., extravagant pay for one person in an organization at the perceived expense of all others, must be avoided.

Adam Smith, the father of free market thinking, believed that free markets also required sympathy, or caring for others and sharing the gains, and that without that there would be a breakdown of the trust on which the market depends for its healthy operation. Moreover, Darwinian thinking is associated with the processes that create self-sustaining ecological systems, not simply the survival of the powerful for a brief period. Think of this as having equity and fairness in the pay structure so that the business system has a greater probability for survival and sustainability.

We believe that you have a fiduciary duty to diligently work toward the best interests of the company in applying these principles. How can we be a high performance organization if 99% of the people don't believe they share equitably in the success of the company? It's your responsibility to assure that they do.

We hope this has been thought provoking, and that you will take appropriate action to address this issue. The company and its employees deserve no less.

Sincerely,

Thorn Inyurside

Ibyn was so shaken by this letter that he immediately resigned his job as CEO and went to Tibet to become a disciple of the Dali Lama, leaving all his worldly goods.

You don't really believe that happened do you?

No, Ibyn continued to rationalize his pay, like most CEOs and boards of directors, much to the detriment of the company. Morale and its related motivation continued to decline, albeit slowly, along with the performance of the company. Ibyn retired just after the company merged with one of its competitors (actually it was bought, but a merger was more palatable to Ibyn's ego). Subsequently, as you might expect, the company went through a series of layoffs and restructuring, raising the share price, and since Ibyn still had a few options from the merger, he profited handsomely, all the while several thousand of his employees fell on harder times.

The Lessons: 1) Pay for everyone, including the CEO, must be internally equitable and externally competitive. 2) Life isn't fair, but it's fairer to executives than to ordinary folks.

Off-shoring – No Panacea

3

"Damn," Harry Knuckles exclaimed. Harry was an operator at the Bendigo Operation.

"What?" responded his buddy, Brit Lyte, having the usual 'deer in the headlights' expression.

"They're shutting Line 3 down, and moving it to China! That line's been running here for nearly 50 years now. How could they do that?" Harry asked to no one in particular.

"Well, I don't work on that line. Good thing," Brit thought aloud, mostly to himself.

"Yeah, but who's next? They've been doing so much down-sizing, right-sizing, out-sourcing, and off-shoring in this company. You just might be next, along with me. Where the hell is it going to end?" Harry lamented.

"Well, the company has to make money," Brit observed, again to no one in particular. It was as if they were having separate, but connected, conversations, each in their own little world.

"We're making money, damn it! You were at the latest quarterly meeting with the general manager," Harry nearly shouted, looking Brit square in the eyes.

"I guess it's not enough," Brit responded laconically, but continued, more insightfully, "You know, when we buy things, we buy the cheapest thing that meets our needs. That puts pressure on prices, which puts pressure on costs, and so our productivity has to go up to lower our costs."

Maybe there was a brighter light on the inside than was obvious on the outside.

"It's enough to give the CEO a huge bonus, while we lose our jobs, or get piddling raises," Harry continued, his temperature apparently rising. It wasn't apparent that he heard Brit's second statement about price and cost pressure and the need for greater productivity.

"Well, that's life," Brit replied with a fatalistic tone.

Harry left the room in a huff.

Meanwhile, in the CEO's office, a secret meeting was in progress. The secret was that the production on Line 3 was being moved to China.

"What does your analysis look like?" Ima Darling, the CEO, asked, while looking intently at Werkin Knumbres, the CFO.

Werkin was thinking to himself just before the meeting began that he hadn't actually completed the analysis, and was still missing some key information, something he was sure Ima didn't want to hear. He had to make a long list of assumptions and caveats regarding wages here and in China, inflation rates, foreign exchange rates, capital and startup costs, travel costs, inventory costs, quality, time to achieve full production, etc. He hadn't even included a mention of certain broader risks related to workforce quality, supply chain issues, local permitting, bureaucracy and politics, as well as the broader issues of geopolitical and economic stability, or lack thereof, but then he'd dismissed those with the thought that Ima was a smart man and could figure those out easily enough.

One bigger issue that really concerned him was the issue of ownership. This deal apparently allowed the local Chinese authorities to take a 50% ownership position in the company, and provide most of the employees, even though the company was providing half of the investment capital and ALL of the intellectual knowledge about building and running an operation like this one.

Werkin was thinking to himself, "Who owns the intellectual property – the patents for the products and the confidential processes for making the product? The Chinese weren't known for their respect for intellectual property rights. Where would all this be in 10-20 years?" He just wasn't sure the company had its eyes fully open to all the issues, since the focus had been getting cheaper labor to allow making cheaper, more competitive products; and getting into the larger markets in China.

"Maybe it's worth it," he thought, "but there's just a huge amount of uncertainty."

"Werkin, are you with us?" Ima asked quizzically.

"Oh, sorry," Werkin said in a slightly startled voice, "There's a lot to consider in the analysis, and I was just going through some of the points in my mind."

"How 'bout we put some of this analysis out of your mind and into the open?" Ima replied curtly. He was not known for his patience. His style was often intimidating to most of his staff.

Werkin went through the assumptions and data, offering his analysis as it currently stood, avoiding the broader strategic issues he had been puzzling over as the meeting began. As he was nearing the end, Ima interrupted.

"So, you're saying we will only make about 50% more net profit, even though direct labor costs fully burdened with overhead have dropped from $35 an hour to $5 an hour? I was expecting more, given that we're fairly labor intensive," Ima questioned the analysis.

Ima took and deep breath, and began, "Well, direct labor is a large part of our costs, in the range of 15-20%, and so that area does improve dramatically. But, we still need to have our managers there to get things going, and then manage the plant, and at their current salaries, plus all the travel and living allowances, which nearly doubles the management component of our labor costs. When you add on what's actually the larger portion of our costs which are in capital, which is larger with the new plant; raw material, which is only slightly cheaper, and energy, which is about the same; and inventory and shipping costs into the US and European markets, then the direct labor advantage drops pretty quickly."

Taking a breath, and continuing, while he had the chance, "And, I've made the assumptions that the quality of our products in the new operation will be on a par with existing operations; and shipping disruptions to our customers will be minimal. The quality at this operation is likely to take a few years to achieve our current standard, given what we've been through here with our quality effort the past few years."

Pausing to let all this sink in, Werkin then continued, "This is my analysis over the next 3-5 years, and there's considerable risk in this prognostication. We'll have to be on top of this on a regular basis during that period. It's really difficult to say where we might be in 10-20 years."

"None of us know where we'll be in 10 years," responded Ima dismissively. "What are the upside and downside scenarios?"

"On the downside, we'll sink $100 million into a venture that returns nothing," Werkin started.

Ima held up his hand, and interrupted, "A reasonable downside, damn it, and upside! I know we could lose it all in the worst case."

Werkin hesitated just a bit, and then proceeded to offer his view on the positive and negative side of factors like sales volume, wage inflation, exchange rate fluctuations, competitive pressures, energy and raw material costs, and so on. In the end he concluded, that a realistic downside would be a negative impact on profits of -50%; and on the upside a positive impact of +200%, with a nominal expected improvement of 50%. "But," he cautioned, "This is our first venture into this type of business, so there are a lot of unknowns."

Whether Ima heard Werkin's last remark, or had considered this point already, is not clear. His next statement was "So, the upside is much higher than the downside, right?"

"Yes, but this isn't a statistically weighted analysis of risks and probabilities," Werkin replied nerdily.

"Let's go ahead with it," Ima instructed Werkin, along with the others in the "secret" meeting, that is, the VP's of capital projects, operations, procurement and HR.

One Year Later

"What? Another problem with startup?" exclaimed Acosta Lott, the project manager for the expansion in China.

"Yeah," replied Jose Frustrado, "Remember we couldn't get the right parts in for the stamping machine, because of shipping problems and customs delays, and so we decided to use the local supplier's so-called equivalent?"

"Un-huh," nodded Acosta, rolling his eyes, "and they failed," he said fatalistically.

"Almost immediately, crappy material, but they were *cheap*," sighed Jose, obviously frustrated, emphasizing the word cheap.

"When can we expect the right parts?" Acosta asked automatically, not expecting a particularly good answer.

"The problem is we just don't know. We've been expecting them for three weeks now, and we keep being told any day. The bureaucracy here is just horrendous. Every time we think we've solved one problem, we run into another – permits, fees, licenses, paperwork, delays – it's just incredible," Jose exclaimed.

The problems continued, and eventually the project was nine months late, and $20M over budget, before getting to reasonable production levels, though still 20% below projected. The problems were numerous, but not unusual or even, some would say, unanticipated. Design delays and design problems occurred as the plant was being designed, due in part to the bureaucracy of getting all the local approvals and doing related changes before construction.

Construction was delayed due to delays in getting the equipment, in part because of supply chain problems, and in part because of customs and import restrictions; and because of a lack of quality workers being available in a timely manner, whose wages had since gone 10% higher than budgeted. Of course, the usual delays occurred during startup as problems were worked out. Acosta Lott retired after the project was turned over. This was his last hurrah, and it really took a toll on his mind and body. Jose Frustrado returned to Mexico, his native country, where, as he explained, "Life is so much simpler and the bureaucracy is even easier, if you can believe that. At least here I speak my native language."

Three Years Later

The problems continued. Wage inflation took its toll on the anticipated profits. Energy costs skyrocketed, along with some of the key raw materials. Supply problems for raw material and spare parts also took its toll. It seemed someone always needed something extra, or a piece of paper signed, before they could get anything delivered. Inventory carrying costs were also much more than was anticipated. It seemed they had to keep about 40% more "in the pipeline" to make sure they could deliver on time to their customers, given all the international shipping and paperwork requirements.

Perhaps the biggest issue of all related to quality problems. In spite of the continued wage inflation, great difficulty was encountered in recruiting, training and developing people, particularly in getting the concept of "quality is job one" embedded into their thinking, and following standard procedures in doing the work.

Perhaps it was a language problem, perhaps a cultural problem (quality had never been a priority for many of the workers), perhaps other issues were involved. Remember Werkin observing how long getting quality embedded into the organization's thinking had taken? And, now you're trying to do it in a foreign country that had little history of applying quality principles.

Four Years Later

At that point, the Chinese venture had sucked the company dry. Profits were down 75% from before the venture was launched, with all the cost over-runs, and continuing problems with operations and product quality. So much for the upside being higher than the downside. Ima Darling announced his retirement early that year, in part it can be surmised for not having achieved all the promised growth and profitability with the new venture.

His replacement, Fan Tastik, had only been on board a month, when he announced that the company was bringing the production back to the US, where things were more predictable, workers more productive, supply chain issues more easily resolved, and quality much higher.

This announcement was met with much pleasure from Harry Knuckles and Brit Lyte, who observed "Maybe it wasn't cheaper after all over there. Labor ain't the only cost that goes into a product." Smart man, that Brit.

A few month later the Chinese announced they were keeping the plant open, under new Chinese ownership. With everything they had learned about the production process and the products, they believed they could handle it now.

The Lesson: Looking at the whole picture usually gives you a better idea of what's happening in the picture.

Core Competency, or Not?

4

Some years ago, a great company named Yarrawonga decided that it needed to reduce costs. So, it sent an announcement out asking everyone for their good ideas on how to reduce costs. Unfortunately, along with the announcement came a set of fixed objectives about how much costs must be reduced, along with some "suggestions" on how to do this.

One suggestion was to convert employees who were considered to be low "value-adding" from being employees to being contractors. After all, they weren't part of the so-called "core competencies" for the company, so who would really miss them. Everyone (in management) thought this was a really good idea, especially the consulting company Weebeesmart, that had suggested it to management in the first place. After all, these people didn't add much value. They were part of a mid-skill labor pool. And, while they didn't make huge salaries, their overhead expenses were really high – health insurance, life insurance, vacation and holidays, and so on- Whew!

"What a really good idea to contract these people out," thought Joe King, CEO of Yarrawonga.

So, they forecast their savings through contracting, and proceeded to work with Weebeebodies, a contractor company, to transfer the employment of all these non-core, low value-adding employees (low value employees?) to the contractor. And, indeed, costs did come down... for a while... but not for long... maybe a year... maybe not..., and then they began to rise again, substantially.

Within a year of contracting out all these non-value add, non-core competency people, the management found they didn't have any qualified people to fill first line supervisor and junior management positions. For you see, these had previously been filled by these so-called non-core competency people who were looking for a longer term career, and had shown that they really could add value at a higher level.

Unfortunately, the elimination of the career path, also eliminated those who had a desire for a career. Some of course only wanted part time employment. Others, being the good, dedicated employees that wanted a career, went about finding a more permanent position, one where they could add increasing value with time, and be recognized for that. That left the pool full of happy part timers and temps, but one that was pretty thin for potential first line supervisors. Those who had left had already decided that the company had little loyalty to them, so why reciprocate. Anyway, they left... for greener (higher value adding) pastures.

Ah, but it gets worse, because Yarrawonga also thought it could save even more money by dismantling all the infrastructure for training and development for these low value adding employees, there was no other venue for getting qualified people ready for the next level up.

Alas, costs for hiring first line supervisors and junior managers increased dramatically. They had to go outside and paid a premium for hiring, both in recruitment, and in the salaries they had to pay to attract others to the company. And this didn't even count the hidden costs for time lost in the transition, and poor morale. So, the cost saving effort actually increased costs. Robert Burns said it best – "The best laid plans o' mice and men gang aft aglay"

Yarrawonga is still competitive, that is, they have competitive parity, since many of their competitors also did the same group think thing, but Joe King may have learned a lesson in all this. He is now much more prone to ask "What do I give up down the road? What do I gain down the road? How does this affect the system, long term? Short term?

The Lesson: Consider the long term consequences to your decisions. Specifically, consider what the people may do in response to the strategy.

Jobs – A Consequence of Being Competitive

5

Webenherr Decads, was a long standing company in the region, founded some 70 years ago by a German, Webenherr, and a Swede, Decads, perhaps an unlikely pair, but one that had worked well from the beginning.

Webenherr took great pride in craftsmanship and engineering, while Decads was more focused on running the business, taking a longer term view on most things, but still recognizing you have to cash flow the business. Over time, the culture had become one that reflected their frugality and craftsmanship, and that was reasonably generous to the employees. Unfortunately, all these years later it was under intense pressure from foreign competition, a flat market for its products, increasing labor costs, increasing energy and material costs, and the ever-present notion that customers tend to buy the cheapest thing that meets their needs, driving prices down. This was particularly true at the Hinder plant, where Sol Licitous was plant manager. With this in mind, we'll now join Harry Helbint and Stew Shoppard at the plant.

 "What's this?" Harry Helbint, the union president sneered, as he read a memo regarding benefits from the plant manager, Sol Licitous.

One of the shop stewards, Stew, was standing nearby, "Oh, it says that sick leave, vacation, and holidays may be reduced by a combined total of 10 days per year."

Helbint cut him off, "I can read damn it. Who said we agreed to this?"

Stew, went on "I don't think we…"

Helbint cut him off again, "I know we didn't agree to it. Stop answering my dumb questions."

"Well, stop asking dumb questions, and I won't answer them," Stew squawked.

Helbint took a deep breath and went storming off toward the plant manager's office. Seething, he could barely contain himself, thinking, "How could they do this? We didn't agree to this. What's going on? I'm going to get to the bottom of this, or we'll go on strike if we can't get this resolved. There are just too many things going on here that aren't good for the membership."

When he arrived at the Sol's office, the door was closed and the secretary was out. So he fidgeted and steamed while he waited. When the door finally opened, the sales manager, Sal Ubrious, a normally gregarious fellow, walked out, looking pretty dour and without so much as a grunt toward Helbint. This distracted Helbint from his original mission,

"What that was all about," he wondered. But, he regained his intent as he walked into Sol's office.

"What's this?" he demanded.

"What's what?" responded Sol staring at the memo.

"You know damn well what this is…" Helbint responded.

"Then why are you asking me what it is?" intoned Sol.

"Don't be catty with me," Helbint said, pulling himself up to his full rotund stature of 5'6". Sol was a lanky 6'6", so Helbint always had to strut just a bit to compensate for the difference.

Sol put his head down, "I'm sorry, but I'm just a bit distracted right now. We just lost a big order. It's about 10% of our total volume. Not big margins, but we cover a lot of our overhead costs with it. A foreign competitor undercut us and they gave the business to them."

Unrelenting, Helbint, said "Is that why you cut our benefits without even talking with me?"

"No, Helbint, look at the top, and bottom, of the memo. See where it says DRAFT; and see where it says we're *considering* any number of options to try to lower our costs, one of which *might be* benefits such as sick leave," Sol said, trying to remain calm, in spite of Helbint's militant attitude. "And, besides, this was a memo to my staff, and not to be distributed to everyone. We've got to get our costs down. That order we just lost was based on cost. The competition got the order because *their prices were lower than our costs*, and didn't leave any room to cover marketing, or G&A or R&D. But back to your question, I understand that we can't cut benefits without negotiating with you and your members. I was just brainstorming with my staff. How'd you get that memo anyway?"

"That doesn't matter. I'm spun up now," Helbint diverted the question.

"Well, while you're here, let's have a serious conversation," Sol offered, finishing with "Off the record. *Pretend* we're friends having a beer."

He emphasized the word pretend, since there was a strict policy against any form of alcohol or drugs on site; and there was a pretty militant relationship between the union and management.

Sol looked at him, "You want a soda?"

"No, thank you," Helbint responded more formally. He was still mad.

"You may have seen this data before, but have a look," Sol flipped some charts up on the wall where he'd been talking with the sales manager. Overall unit costs had been climbing about 4% per year, for labor and raw material, but particularly for energy. But prices had actually declined about 1% per year for several years. Margins were dropping markedly, leaving just enough to cash flow the business and leaving barely enough to cover marketing and G&A, let alone R&D and profit. "We're in a pretty serious situation here, and we need your help to address this deteriorating position."

"Am I supposed to believe this? You sure this isn't some fabricated story to leverage us out of our benefits and wages?" Helbint asked.

"Yes, you're supposed to believe this, and no these aren't fabricated. They're an accurate reflection of our situation, and it's not sustainable," insisted Sol.

"So, you want the membership to take it in the ass on their wages and benefits?" responded Helbint, less than subtly.

"No, not really. I'm just giving you data right now. We have to lower our costs if we're going to survive. One way to do that is to become more productive – the same wages for a higher level of output. Another is to reduce benefits. There are other options – look at the draft memo you have.

You know as well as I do that our health care costs have skyrocketed over the past five years, but the deductible is the same. Our energy costs have also skyrocketed, but our work rules are the same, and our productivity hasn't really budged. It's just not sustainable," Sol said, somewhat randomly, just to illustrate the situation.

"We've worked awfully hard to keep this company going, and for our benefits. The members, including me will not be happy about *any* cut in benefits," Helbint said, putting the emphasis on the word any. "Besides, they're never going to close this plant, they've got too much invested, and we're the key supplier, maybe only supplier, for one of our downstream sister plants just two miles away. They can't afford to shut us down."

Sol was quietly thinking, "There it was again, the 'they' word, as if some mysterious 'they' in the sky made all the decisions affecting the business with little consideration for the people in the plant." This really frustrated him. He calmed himself.

"No, Helbint, it's not your work ethic that's the problem, it your work rules that are making us less productive, *and less competitive*," Sol emphasized, continuing, "If we aren't competitive there aren't any jobs for anyone, including me, and '*they*' don't have jobs either."

"We negotiated those work rules fair and square to protect our jobs and make sure the members weren't taken advantage of by the management," Helbint pointed out.

"Yes, and when they were negotiated, it was probably the right thing to do," replied Sol, trying to strike a conciliatory tone.

He hesitated to point out that management had caved in to many of the demands for fear of a strike, which continued to be a constant threat, often voiced by Helbint, so he had to be careful with his statements. "I don't have an issue per se with your wages and benefits, but if they come at a price that makes us non-competitive, then there may not be *any* wages or benefits for anyone." He kept hammering on this point, but was the message being understood by Helbint?

"Bullcrap," responded Helbint, so apparently not.

"Just give me some examples of what you think us union members should be doing," Helbint went on.

Sol began, "Well, here's one - right now call-ins are expensive, and we have a lot of them. For example, we pay for four hours per call-in at time and a half, even if the person only works an hour. Here's another, operators could do some routine care and PM for the equipment, but the work rules have been interpreted such that they don't touch machinery except to operate it, even if it's something as simple as tightening a screw."

Pausing briefly, he went on, "Electricians could loosen hold-down bolts on motors, but right now they have to wait for a mechanic. Oh, and we pay them to wait. And, right now all mechanics have to have a helper, even when they don't need help. I could go on, but to me all these rules are just silly," lamented Sol, realizing too late that it would have been better to have omitted that last phrase about being silly.

"Well that's only fair to be paid for a call-in, and those other things, we're just trying to protect jobs," Helbint responded firmly, as if he were speaking to his members right now.

"I'm not suggesting that it's fair or unfair, and you're right, those things are in the contract, and we have to honor that contract," Sol said, continuing his effort to be conciliatory. "But the fact is, those kinds of rules make things cost more, and make us less competitive, and they *put your jobs at risk,*" Sol emphasized.

"Let me try to explain in a different way," Sol pleaded. "When you go buy things and you're having difficulty in making a decision, because the products available as far as you can tell, are comparable, which one do you buy?"

Helbint gave him a stern look, frowning.

"The cheapest?" Sol went on.

"No, I wouldn't," responded Helbint somewhat hostilely.

"What then?"

"I'd buy the one made in America," Helbint puffed his chest up a little.

"Well your wife wouldn't," Sol suggested.

"Yep, we've had that talk," acknowledged Helbint, sheepishly.

Sol smiled broadly, almost bursting into laughter, and continued, "Look you *should* buy those things that are made in this country. I do too, particularly when the costs are very close. But, most folks buy the cheapest thing that meets their needs. They're not willing to pay much of a premium for 'made in America', or whatever country they're in.

That's why Walmart is so successful, and that's also why prices are always under pressure. And, that's why costs are always under pressure. And, that's why we've got to offset that pressure with improved productivity."

Sol, though frustrated, and still not sure if he was making any headway with Helbint, continued with another example, "Let's pretend you're going to take your car for a tune up. Knowing a little about cars, you want to make sure the job is done right, so you watch what's going on. Out comes the mechanic, along with his helper, who opens the hood. The mechanic peers in, looking inquisitively, and says 'Well, it looks like we're going to have to unhook the wires, so I'll need an electrician; and it looks like we'll have to loosen the hoses, so I'll need a pipefitter for that; and the electronics need to be checked for calibration, so I'll need an electronics tech as well.' While they're waiting for these specialists, the helper and mechanic just watch while all that gets done. When that's done, the mechanic changes the plugs and adjusts a few things, and then waits for the same technicians to reverse the process. *Would you be willing to pay for all that?* It would probably triple your cost, out of your pocket. Or, would you be like me and expect the mechanic to take care of it all, and pay him a good wage? Which scenario would be more competitive, and which one would you be willing to pay for?"

Helbint was clearly irritated by the analogy, and apparently felt ambivalent, and trapped, in his reply, "Well if it made for better quality or safety, I'd pay for it." The company had a long standing policy for excellence in quality and safety, so this was the only "out" that Helbint could think of.

"Really?" Sol starred at Helbint intently. He thought he might have him convinced.

"This is all just bullcrap," Helbint abruptly stood up and walked out, repeating, "Just bullcrap."

Sol had given it his best shot. In subsequent negotiations, the union barely budged, notwithstanding the analogies and cajoling. Their constant refrain was twofold: 1) We're not going to take a pay cut; 2) Work rules protect jobs; and 3) They're never going to shut this place down, because they've got too much invested here supporting the sister plant down the road.

The next year the Hinder plant was closed, and the sister plant was restructured under more favorable, productive, and competitive terms.

The Lessons: 1) If your work rules make you less competitive you put everyone's job at risk. 2) Being competitive in the market place requires productivity to improve year on year.

Disappearing Markets

6

"Wow, would you look at that!" marveled Amy Skeptik, one of the mid-level managers at Numurkah Company. She was impressed by the new technology that made digital imaging possible. Almost immediately though, she thought out loud, "Wonder how this is going to go down in film processing"

"Oh, they'll love it, it just means that people will take more pictures and have them processed using our labs and printed on the paper we make," replied Neb Ulous casually.

"Really? I'd just store the pictures I wanted to keep on my computer and only print the ones that I really wanted to print. How many pictures do you have stored in a box somewhere that you look at once, and then put away, most never to be seen again," suggested Amy.

"Huh," Neb thought out loud, not really understanding the meaning of what Amy had just suggested, continuing with "Nah, this is great stuff, a whole new market, that's complimentary to our current products."

Meanwhile over in marketing a giant battle was going on, with intense feverish debate about the new technology.

"This will destroy our film processing business," Nigel Naysayer, a senior executive, remarked, "we just can't do that."

"Bullcrap, said Moven Forward, the executive responsible for the new digital technology, "it's a whole new market, and the whole world is going digital."

"I notice you've got your new digital mobile phone there," he added, just to emphasize the point.

"We should set up a separate division and get on with this technology." Moven was known as a ladder climber, and clearly wanted to be in charge of a new division with a bright future.

"No," replied Nigel, "If we move ahead with this it needs to be part of film processing. That's where the money is. Not only that, but this technology will develop slowly. People just aren't going to give up their pictures easily."

"Yeah, it'll develop slowly, according to Moore's Law," rebuffed Moven cynically. (Moore's Law says something to the effect that digital technological capability doubles every two years).

The debate raged on.

Meanwhile over in the CEO's office, he was pondering just what to do. He had a so-called Seven Sigma background, and was heavy into quality principles, routinely thinking it could alleviate most problems. Perhaps more importantly, he was unwilling to create a new business unit that could harm another business unit within the company.

So, he decided to license it. And the licensees ran with it, roughly following Moore's Law, and Moven's prediction. Meanwhile, the film processing business declined to a tiny fraction of its former self, and finally into bankruptcy.

The Lesson: Markets rule, not politics. Be constantly aware of shifting market conditions and technologies. Think buggy whips, carburetors, pay telephones, newspapers, books, etc.

Constancy of Purpose Is Essential

7

The Wanadoo operation had spent the past several years in an extensive improvement effort led by the plant manager, Stan Backenwatch, and production manager, Una Nimity, after Stan finally convinced Una that production had a much bigger role to play in making a plant reliable than did maintenance. Una then used a production-led approach to make major improvements in the plant's performance. Unfortunately, with so much improvement, Stan was promoted to a staff role to help the VP of Manufacturing do all the good things he'd done at Wanadoo, and Una was recruited away by another organization, for the same purpose.

Ses Ephus, the maintenance manager, was now sizing up the new managers coming in, thinking to himself "Just more people to train in what we've already learned. Seems like we've done this a hundred times." Ses always felt like he was on a treadmill, never making any real sustained progress.

The new plant manager, Fred Fickle, was very different from Stan Backenwatch, and could change his mind on a dime, going with one approach one minute and then changing direction only a moment later. He seemed typically to be an advocate for the approach of whomever he spoke with last.

The new production manager, Victor Vain, was pretty much enamored with himself and his production management skills.

He was **focused** on production, and little else. Production produced, maintenance maintained, purchasing purchased, and so on. His view was that if everyone just did their job well, things would work fine (ignoring all the task interdependency among the various departments and the need to work together on many issues).

Meanwhile there continued to be pressure from the competition in China, and other parts of the world and of course the US. This put lots of pressure on costs, and likewise on sales. Most managers figured any order was a good order.

Ses met with Fred and Victor to offer them a comprehensive briefing on the current status of the plant's performance, and more importantly, how they had improved performance over the past few years. Both demurred, suggesting that it be done next week when more time was available. Ses agreed, and they set the meeting for the following week.

The next week, Fred postponed, and it was rescheduled. The following week, Victor postponed, and it was rescheduled. The next week both postponed, and it was rescheduled. Ses was getting pretty frustrated, and saw both managers, particularly Victor, seeming to revert to bad old habits. Fred, of course, didn't seem to be able to stick to anything.

Finally, with Ses's insistence they held the meeting. Ses began with the concept of working together, and offering that it had been very effective in working with Dan Driver, the previous production manager.

"This doesn't mean we're going to have to go off into the forest and camp together, and sing Kumbaya, does it?" asked Victor suspiciously.

"No, I'm talking about working together here in the plant, not in the woods," retorted Ses, sensing Victor's suspicion.

"You know, if we all just did our jobs well, we'd be in fine shape," responded Victor, reflecting his long held belief.

"Yes, we all have to do our jobs," interjected Fred, "and we have to work as a team." He'd been to a seminar recently on working as a team, and taking responsibility for your work.

Ses continued with the plant data, "According to our data, some 60% of our production losses aren't related to the equipment breaking down, but things like product changeovers, short stops, rate and quality problems, process fouling, raw material problems, and production planning. And, of the 40% that is equipment related, we're seeing a lot of problems with poor operating practices inducing the failures. We can argue about who caused the failures, but let's say about half of those are because of poor operating practices, that is, not starting up right, not shutting down right, not running the process per the standards, then maintenance only controls about 20% of the problems. Other studies indicate it's only 10%, but I'm willing to accept that it may be twice that."

"Hmmph," Victor grunted in his most cynical tone, "that's big of you."

Ses ignored Victor for the moment and continued "When we started working together to solve problems and support one another, on-time delivery went from 89% to 97%, OEE went from 61% to 72%, scrap and rework were cut in half, and more importantly, unit costs dropped by nearly 10%, creating substantially better gross profits. While these still aren't world class numbers, they much better than before."

"Yeah, and market price dropped another 10% just over the past six months, so what has that bought us?" Victor looked skeptically at Ses.

Ses countered, "Well, we're still in business. Without that, our situation would be much more difficult. We've got to keep improving to stay in business."

It was hard to argue with that, so Victor changed course, "I don't believe the data."

"What? Are you suggesting I've cooked the numbers?" Ses asked incredulously.

Backing off, Victor said "No, but I want to study the data more."

But he never did. Victor also had a passive aggressive streak in him. He had a history of agreeing to do something just to get people off his back, and then not doing it, always coming up with an excuse as to why it hadn't been done. He stuck with his philosophy of production produces and maintenance maintains. He was also incensed when he found that one of the carryovers from previous management was that he was being held accountable for unplanned downtime and maintenance costs; and that Ses was being held accountable for on-time delivery.

Victor called another meeting with Fred. "I'm not responsible for maintenance costs or unplanned downtime," he demanded.

"Of course not! Why are you upset?" Fred responded.

"Look at this report Ses gave me," Victor handed the report to Fred. "See right there where it says 'responsible manager', it's got Ses's name **and** my name," putting emphasis on 'and' as if it were an insult.

Ses tried to explain the logic in this, but Victor would have none of it. And Fred, being the fickle fellow he was, conceded to Victor's demands.

Over time, the plant regressed – on-time delivery deteriorated, as did OEE; and costs began to increase, in spite of additional cost cutting. Eventually, the plant was put on notice that performance had to improve, or else. About this time, and seeing a future that didn't include him, Fred retired. Similarly, Victor became frustrated and went looking for another company that had a better appreciation for a good operations manager.

Ses thought to himself, "I guess we didn't do a good job training that bunch. Maybe the next ones will go better."

The Lesson: Constancy of purpose is essential. Your performance should depend more on your processes than on specific people.

Management Stability – Critical to Success

8

Woolamaloo was viewed as a very good company on Wall Street. It had a good track record, solid balance sheet, and had a reputation for routinely meeting customer expectations for quality and service. Being the enlightened company that it was, it also had a policy of changing operations managers every two years. The prevailing thinking in this policy was that the "rising stars" needed to be exposed to many different areas of the company so they could handle broader responsibilities as they moved up through the corporation. This also included transferring people from one division into another to expose them across the company's different business units. The practice seemed logical enough.

However, as with all companies, Woolamaloo had been under considerable cost pressure in its markets – increasing globalization with supply exceeding demand, customer demands for lower costs, higher raw material costs, higher energy costs, that is, the usual litany of cost pressures.

Jack Avaltrades was a typical manager coming into an operation. He's a Georgia Tech graduate, really top notch, a hard-working, intelligent guy, and on the fast track. He has had several jobs in his 15 years at Woolamaloo, ranging from engineering design to operations to sales.

Now he's been named operations manager at one of their bigger production plants. He's both eager, and a little apprehensive.

Privately he opined "I've never had to deal with managing 400 people. The biggest group I've ever had was only 25." But being the eager-beaver that he was, he took the job with enthusiasm. After all, he was a "rising star".

On his first day as operations manager, there was an accident in one of the operating areas. It seems someone opened a valve when they shouldn't have and sprayed dilute acid on a maintenance employee. Fortunately, no one was seriously injured, but they were "lucky" as the story goes. The next day he was to have an energy audit from corporate, and on Thursday, the VP of operations was coming for a pre-planned visit.

And, his staff were clamoring for decisions about a number of issues that had been sitting for several weeks pending his arrival – the previous manager had left some weeks before, and the interim manager was reluctant to make any significant decisions, other than those essential to keep things going.

One of Jack's staff, Jay Jelus, was also a bit envious. He felt the job of operations manager should be his, since he'd been at the plant for 10+ years, and now here was this "hotdog" coming in from nowhere, knowing nothing about the processes or people. Others were less jaundiced in their view, but not particularly enthusiastic. Sid Sinical, a maintenance supervisor, remarked with obvious disdain, "Just another pretty face in a long line of pretty faces. He'll be gone in two years."

Most of Jack's first day was tied up with the accident with him asking numerous questions -

"Did we have a lockout-tagout procedure to avoid these situations? Was it being followed? Was there a work permit? Who opened the valve anyway? Why would anyone do such a dumb thing? Is the worker OK? How long will he be out? Is this an incident to be reported to OSHA? Who's preparing the report on this? Do we have to do a root cause analysis?"

The next day was spent meeting individually with his staff, and trying understand their goals, problems, and so on, and to make decisions that had been waiting for him, notwith-standing his lack of knowledge about the processes for this operation and the staff's individual capabilities. He had reviewed the introduction on financials, a block diagram of the plant process, and one page bio's of each staff member.

The day after was spent preparing for the visit from his boss, Cal Amity, VP of Operations, all the while answering numerous phone calls from various customers upset about delivery or quality problems, and from his staff responding with their answers to these problems. Apparently an unexpected shutdown two weeks ago had put them behind on nearly every order, what with the new lean manufacturing mantra – minimal inventories. "I didn't think we had any big problems here," he mused. He had yet to walk around the plant and get to know a few of the shop floor people and the overall condition of the equipment. Maybe tomorrow.

Tomorrow came. He met with his boss, Cal, who admonished that the plant had to get its house in order, "Rising raw material and energy costs are just killing us in the market place," he said in an urgent tone, "Besides, remember that big stock buyback we did to deflect that unsolicited offer by Bigbucks Corporation? Well our cash is down to a minimum now, and the banks are getting nervous about our balance sheet. I want a 10% reduction in our fixed costs within the next three months. Send me your draft plan next week."

Then Cal went on to chat about how the move into his new house was going and how the wife and kids were doing settling in, and left.

While Cal was asking these routine questions, Jack was nodding that things were fine, but thinking "There are still dozens of boxes in the garage from the move, and my wife is really frustrated with getting kids adjusted to a new home, school, and friends, none of this made any easier by a whiny teenager really upset over leaving friends 'back home'." He left the plant that day wondering how he was going to break it to his wife that the next few days (weeks?), were going to involve a lot of long hours at work. So much for easing into the job and getting to know the processes and people.

The pressure and seemingly endless long days continued. He managed to cut fixed costs by 10% as demanded by his boss, cutting staff mostly, plus some contractor work, but this resulted in the loss of operating staff to cover for training and related improvement efforts, in further delays to maintenance projects already overdue, in deferrals in training in new processes for the operating staff, and in postponements in minor capital improvement projects, among other lesser things.

And, it had a huge demoralizing effect on the staff. They thought that new management would bring in new ideas and a better work environment and performance. Theirs was short lived optimism.

Added to this were the seeming endless audits – safety, energy, financial, some from corporate, others from state, and still others federal, among many. He just seemed to go from one urgent matter to another.

In spite of all this, he seemed to be doing a reasonable job for the business. The operation was a cost center, not a profit center, and he was generally meeting corporate goals for costs and volume, and though safety performance was not great, it was now in the average range for the company.

Time flew, and before he knew it, his two years were up, and he was being transferred to a commercial job. "Whew, boy is it good to have this over with," he thought, "now I should have a job with less pressure, and be better positioned for the next advance."

Meanwhile, Sid Sinical was wondering who the next pretty face would be, and how long he would last. He felt confident he could outlast the next one as well, irrespective of the direction the new guy wanted to go in. "Managers are like dogs," he thought, "every new one wants to pee on the post and mark its territory, but it's hardly ever the same set of posts. It sure would be nice if they were consistent."

Shortly after Jack left, a new manager was brought in. And shortly after that, the plant had a major accident, an explosion that killed one person, and seriously injured two others. To make a long story short, the explosion had multiple causes – partly because of delays in maintenance to a vessel that had been previously patched, partly because of failure to update procedures related to the process, and partly because of failure to train the operators in the new process configuration. Jack was never held accountable for any of this. He was gone. After all, things were pretty good on his watch.

Time went on with new managers coming and going. During one period of 3 years, they never had the same management team for more than six months, bringing in a new production, or plant, or technical manger every six months. Pressures intensified with each new manager.

Each did the best they could and were typically thankful to be leaving the job of running a plant. The churn continued. The folks on the floor became "webees" – we be here when you be gone. So, we'll not be doing much differently, since it doesn't seem to matter. The operation didn't get any worse in cost performance, but it didn't get any better either. And, with downward pricing pressures, it soon wasn't making sufficient gross profits to re-invest in developing new products and markets. After several years of this vicious cycle, the company closed several operations, sold most of the rest, and became a wisp of its former self.

The Lessons: 1) Changing managers every two years induces misalignment, instability, and re-direction, even in the best companies. 2) An environment of routine cost cutting often makes the situation worse, and can create a 'death spiral'. 3) Managers must be in their positions long enough to suffer the consequences, or reap the rewards, of the decisions they made in the first two years.

Customer Service Taken Too Far

9

Paraburdoo was a really good company, one highly responsive to the markets it served, and really dedicated to customer service. The company worked hard to live by the creed "The customer is always right". This philosophy transcended the organization, and indeed, within the operation, each of the functional groups viewed the others as 'customers'. For example, the marketing and sales was the customer of operations; within operating plants, production was the customer of maintenance. And the corporate mantra was that you worked really hard to keep both your external and your internal customers happy.

Unfortunately, this overall philosophy, while mostly providing good results, could at times, create havoc in the workplace. Makim Happi, VP of Marketing and Sales (sales was his real strength) had developed his career around customer satisfaction, and made lots of promises to customers on price, quality and delivery, even for small orders. But, Makim, didn't really understand the actual costs of production, or the implications of his demands on the plants. Of course, he understood standard costs that were created by the accounting system. But these rarely, if ever, accounted for things like changeover times for a specific product, or maintenance cost implications for difficult-to-run products, or specific energy costs on a given product, as well as other consequential costs that the accounting system just couldn't calculate, and so these were allocated across all the products as overhead. This allocation was a pretty broad brush, and a really big percentage of total cost.

In any event, Makim would routinely call the plants and demand changes to the production schedule to make one customer or another happy. Or, actually one of his lieutenants would usually make the call – 'Makim wants you to get this to customer X, ASAP'.   And, since Paraburdoo was a "market driven company", Makim's authority to make these changes was only challenged at the risk of future un-employment. So, few operations managers risked that undesirable condition.

Moreover, at the plants, the production managers were "King" (or "Queen" as the case might be). And so when they spoke about needing to deliver on product, often at the behest of Makim, everybody jumped up and said 'yes sir', at least in the figurative sense. As you might expect, this often resulted in very reactive practices at the plants – the production schedule changed daily, and the maintenance schedule changed daily.

The truth is, they didn't really have a maintenance schedule. Well, actually they had one, but nobody paid any attention to it, since it was subject to change at a moment's notice. Anyway, on top of all this, the equipment would break down frequently. I suppose that's easy enough to understand, if the maintenance schedule was mostly ignored and so maintenance didn't get done. Below is a common story on how all this played out day-to-day in the plant.

Ann O'Maly (or Queeny as she was sometimes pejoratively called, though never to her face) would often get calls from Makim, or one of his lieutenants, usually "Brownnose."

"Change the production schedule," demanded Browny (his other nick name), "Our biggest customer wants this product on this date and we have to meet it."

"But, but," protested Ann, "that will make us spend a lot of time reconfiguring the equipment and changing the production templates. That will be really expensive."

"Excuses, excuses, is that all you know how to do down there? I don't care. This is straight from Makim and he's demanding we get this done now," continued Browny.

Ann, being keen to keep her employment with the company, groused a bit, but finally agreed, "All right, we can do it, but it will impact these orders..." then listing them for Browny.

"That's not acceptable," retorted Browny, "you've got to do better than that."

"We can, but that will require extra shifts, and lots of overtime," responded Ann.

"That's your problem. Now git'er done," Browny responded contemptuously. Browny was a fan of the Cable Guy.

So Ann called her supervisors to explain the new requirements. "But, the machine we use to make that product is down for maintenance," Tad Pole practically shouted, "we've been patching that thing for months now, and we finally had the time to do it right, and now you're saying you need it back on line pronto."

"Yes," Ann said emphatically, "Yes!" again just for good measure.

"But, but," protested Tad, "we're right in the middle of doing the work. What would you like me *not* to do to get it back to you?"

"That's your problem," Ann sneered and was clearly becoming annoyed, "I need it back by midnight tonight so the late shift can get on this, so we can meet Makim's delivery."

"Crap," responded Fester Sore, one of the mechanics, "how 'bout you just go out there and fix it yourself then, if you need it that much." A long silence ensued.

"Just get it back by midnight," Ann demanded, and left.

Tad is now thinking, "Crap, I can't get all the work done, let alone, run it through some trials to test it out and commission it." Tad had just been through a reliability review where they had stressed that the highest risk of failure was during startup, and where they had said to fix things right – restore them to like new performance before turning them back over to production. He'd been patching this machine for months, just to keep it running. And now, he'd have to do things the same old way, with the same old results.

So he did, and true to form, the machine broke again, before the delivery was completed for the customer. And, they went through the same scenario described above… twice. The production was finally completed and they made the delivery just in time that Makim, and Ann, had demanded. And kudos went out to all, especially Tad, for getting things back on line. After all, they were customer driven, and they had yet again delivered to the customer.

But, other customer deliveries suffered, and somehow, Tad didn't feel totally good about this. He appreciated the "attaboys", but he'd like more "attaboys" for doing things right, not doing them over.

The Lessons: 1) Taking any principle to an extreme, like customer service, without looking at the overall performance of the system, will likely result in poorer performance.

Reducing Hiring Times – A Misguided Approach

10

Toolonga Corporation was growing fairly quickly with the introduction of several new products that had been well received in the market place. As a result, of course, it was hiring at a rapid rate to support that growth. Unfortunately, however, it was losing people almost as rapidly as it was able to hire them. It seems that all the "baby boomers" working for the company were now becoming "elder boomers", and retiring.

Their consultants, Weebeesmart (yes, again– they get around!) in an effort to help accelerate the hiring process came up with the idea of reducing the cycle time for hiring. In addition, they had recently developed a new improvement program – Seven Sigma. After all, the reasoning went, if Six Sigma was good, then Seven Sigma must be better, and the consultant thought that the hiring process was ripe for the use of Seven Sigma to make improvements.

Incidentally, the consultant had recently trained several of their young employees in Seven Sigma and so they wanted to try to make use of this new tool to help their clients get better, and maybe, just maybe, earn some fees from the investment. Never mind that Toolonga was growing so rapidly that it typically operated at Three Sigma in most of its processes. Weebeesmart had also encouraged them to get everybody involved in improvement, and the idea of reducing the hiring cycle time had come from the HR manager. So, clearly it was a good idea.

Unfortunately, Toolonga didn't have enough staff to do the Seven Sigma analysis of hiring process and cycle times and so they hired Weebeesmart., which also had a sister recruiting organization (they were well versed in Human Resource Management). So they involved their sister company in helping with the analysis- they were only a tiny bit farther afield from the guys working directly with Toolonga.

In any event the analysis proceeded and a key result was that the cycle time for the initial recruiting period was pretty long – finding the right people in the right places took the longest average time, and also had the greatest variation. That's what the data said. So, the reasoning went, we need to address this most urgently, and it will help us hire more people more quickly and support our growth. So they developed an action plan and implemented the new approach. They used their extensive data base to analyze the appropriate demographics and identify areas for potential recruits who had the requisite skills to support their growth.

Things went swimmingly, for a while. Recruits were being brought in at a much more rapid rate, job openings were being filled, indoctrination of new people had been accelerated, and it seemed the problem was solved- very few open slots stayed that way for long. Did I mention that Weebeesmart also earned a fee on each new recruit?

Unfortunately, this new approach was less selective in picking the best people from the available talent pool, so many either washed out sooner, or in some cases managed to do an adequate job, but not a superior job. The net result was a higher turnover rate, and less competent first line supervisors. But, since that had a fast process for recruiting and replacing the people, the vacated jobs were in fact filled more quickly.

All this resulted in higher training costs for each new recruit, but this too had been accelerated, though not much consideration had been given to the quality of the result of the more rapid training. The veteran supervisors also had to spend more time helping the new people, and less time taking care of customers. Sometimes , it just takes time for people to learn their jobs. The practice part is often more important than the training part of learning.

As a result of lower standards resulting from the new less skilled people, and more time being spent by the veterans helping the new people, they spent less time for taking care of the company's problems. This all resulted in the company providing poorer customer service, and more complaints about the quality of their work. Sadly, this also resulted in some orders being terminated, though not the big ones. Toolonga's growth rate slowed, to the point of being jokingly called Tooshorta. And the original problem had solved itself.

The Lessons: 1) Be careful that improving a system in one area does not have an overall negative effect on the business. 2) Many systems are self-correcting.

The Huntin' Dog and The Kennel Dog

11

Kakado was a good company. They were well respected in their industry, had extensive and long standing relationships with major customers. They took great pride in all their policies and practices. One policy in particular that was viewed as quite good was that for selecting plant managers in their manufacturing operations.

Their plant managers were selected using a very extensive process – standard testing for personality types, comprehensive review of educational background, performance reviews, background checks, current performance, upward appraisal results and so on. Though many of these reviews were a bit superficial.

Ibe Bold was a particularly well respected plant manager, at least by the higher ups. He made excellent presentations; schmoozed exceptionally well with the bosses; routinely talked with the employees; made the rounds in the local community clubs. He was clearly a top manager.

One day the wizard from the corporate office, Ima Seagull, came to the plant to do a review of the plants' operating practices. He was impressed when he walked around. Everything seemed pretty clean and tidy. All the procedures seemed in order. But, performance at the plant was just not what it should be, given all the things that seemed in order.

So, being the good corporate dooby that he was, he began probing a little more deeply into the issues facing the plant. He talked with several operators and mechanics about how things were going.

Seagull asked "What do you think of Bold?"

"What do you mean what do I think? Think about what?" responded Sue Pervisor, an operating group leader.

"Oh, about the way he manages the plant, in general," said Seagull.

"Humph, he talks a good game", answered Sue, "but he sure is quick to change his mind when a new directive comes down from you guys at corporate. One week this is the priority, the next week that is the priority, the next week another thing is the priority. After a few weeks of this, we've all pretty much just decided to sit back wait, 'til it changes again. There's a lot less hassle and frustration that way, but not much gets done." Sue went on "We just figure it out for ourselves based on what we think is important, and that usually works pretty well. We figure we'll be here when he's gone, so there's not too much need to get excited about what he says."

Seagull was puzzled, "What do you mean when you say 'that usually works pretty well'? The plant's performance is pretty ordinary."

Sue was clearly annoyed, "Yeah, but it'd be a lot worse if we went chasing every rabbit Bold sees. At least we do what we can as well as we can."

"Well, thanks for your time Sue", said Seagull, clearly wanting to get away quickly.

This whole conversation had made him very uncomfortable, given all the stellar reports he'd received from the bosses about what an up and coming manager Bold was. "He's better at managing his career than he is at managing the plant," he thought to himself.

Undeterred, Seagull went on to interview a few more people, including Manny, a veteran mechanic who was highly regarded in the company – good skills, hard worker, never any disciplinary problems, and a straight talker. As with Sue, Seagull asked Manny "What do you think of Bold?"

Without hesitating Manny replied quietly, but firmly "Kennel dog."

"Kennel dog?" questioned Seagull.

"Yeah, kennel dog. You do any huntin' Mr. Seagull?"

"No, not really." replied Seagull. "Well if you did, you'd know the difference between a kennel dog and a huntin' dog. Bold there's a kennel dog. He looks good in a kennel – pretty coat, well behaved, no scars anywhere, all the right markings… but, he can't hunt. Not worth a damn out huntin'."

Seagull was still a bit perplexed at the analogy, but beginning to understand. He decided to ponder all this for a while, continuing with the more technical details of his review.

The very next week he was at another plant, one where the plant manager didn't get particularly good reviews from the bosses.

The plant manager, I.M. Boring, wasn't considered to be very good on his feet – not as articulate as some, typically thought long and hard before answering questions, at times offered too many options as answers, and generally left senior management frustrated at his communications skills. He wasn't very handsome either, tall and lanky with a face that yes, only a mother could love, and his dress definitely was not out of GQ. Senior management preferred bold, decisive managers that came up with clear solutions. Some wondered how Boring ever came to be a plant manager.

But, the plant's performance was quite good. Some thought he was jiggering the numbers; others thought he was just lucky; still others said he had structural advantages – a good, non-union workforce, low power costs, etc.

So Seagull decided to do a similar exercise as he had done at Bold's plant, and talk to the people doing the work about their impressions of Boring.

He first talked with Fay Bulous, a long time operator within the plant. "What do you think of Boring and the way he runs the plant?" he asked.

Looking a little quizzical, Fay slowly offered "Well, he's been here a long time, and knows the people and processes pretty well. I've never been able to put one over on him, not that I would try. He's always been respectful of what I do. I did hear he almost got fired a year ago for doing something dumb with the higher ups. I don't know the details. He pretty much does what he says he's going to do. Once he came back to us to tell us that he wouldn't be able to do something he'd already promised. Most managers wouldn't take the time."

Seagull was intrigued by Fay's ramblings. "So, do you think the people on the floor respect him?"

"Oh, for sure. I think most of us would like him to stay as long as he can. He can be demanding, and he's not much flash, and he bumbles about sometimes, but he works really hard to support us in meeting his demands; he talks to us on the floor, and tries to eliminate obstacles, and answers our questions honestly; he gets us the training we need as best he can; yeah, I think most folks here think highly of him."

Hesitating, "Oh yeah, one other thing, he tries to filter all the crap that's coming down from HQ all the time, so that we're focused on doing the few important things," added Fay.

"Do you hunt Fay?" asked Seagull.

"No, but I do fish some. Why?" she responded.

"Just curious," said Seagull as he left for corporate headquarters to give senior management a full report.

The Lesson: A good huntin' dog may not look pretty, but gets the job done; a kennel dog may look pretty in the kennel, but he won't do you any good in the field. Do you have huntin' dogs or kennel dogs running your operation?

An Aging Workforce – A Crisis in Waiting

12

Baby boomers will soon be retiring by the millions, putting an increasing burden on our social services. Perhaps as importantly, this will reduce the number of skilled workers available to do the jobs that need to be done. It's a double whammy.

"Did you hear?" asked Tim Newby, a youngish veteran, who had been working for Dumberning Corporation for 10 years now.

"Hear what?" asked Will Tuffenuff, a real veteran in the workforce, having been with the company for nearly 40 years.

"Old Ben Codger is retiring," Tim offered, "I didn't think he'd ever retire. He did say he might be willing to work some after his retirement, just not full time. I think his wife wants him home more."

"Good for him," said Will, thinking wistfully about his own dashed hopes for retirement, "I can't really retire right now. Wish I could, but I've got too many debts, and not enough saved. I reckon I'll have to carry on, 'til I drop or I'm forced to quit. Lots of other folks seem to be in the same boat – kids in college, second mortgages, too much debt and not enough savings. I reckon there'll be lots of other people just like me. I just read that half the people in the country that are retirement age, or soon will be, can't retire, because they don't have enough money saved."

"I hear they're re-starting the apprenticeship program," Tim said softly, almost to himself, but trying to avoid Will's obvious discomfort.

"Oh," Will's wistful thinking was abruptly interrupted, "Yeah, I've heard that too, but right now they've only got two apprentices in it. They must not be too serious about it," Will said, with only a tiny bit of sarcasm in his voice, "They're dabbling to give the *appearance* of progress, while avoiding the problem. The big boss isn't about to hire a lot more people with the economy so weak." Will had the wisdom of his age.

"Oh," Tim said weakly, "What are we going to do when Ben leaves? He's the only one that has a really good understanding of a lot of the machines around here."

"Others will have to learn, and likely make a lot of mistakes along the way," Will responded, observing the obvious.

"Doesn't sound too smart to me," Tim thought out loud, "Don't you think it would be a good idea to have training programs and procedures that help us to do what Ben can do?"

"Good idea, but nobody seems to care much," Will countered, "They just don't want to spend the money on people, or training, or developing procedures. We'll pay for it later though. Sure enough, as we muddle through, but everybody else seems to be doing this, so I guess we won't be at any disadvantage."

Meanwhile, in Dumberning's corporate HR's department, Bea Pleasant, the HR manager, was meeting with the CEO, Al Betmejob, and CFO, Hafner Headengrund, to review the most recent demographics data and its implications.

She began, "Our demographics are becoming an even more serious problem. The average age of our workforce is nearly 50 now, and over the next five years, nearly a quarter of them will be eligible to retire at full benefits. It's not like we didn't see this coming. And we still haven't begun any significant recruiting effort to hire and train any new people. Speaking of training, our training is seriously underfunded. Even our apprentice program is weak." Looking at Haf, "Didn't you say our pension fund was still underfunded by several million?"

Al and Haf looked at each other, as if to roll their eyes, and both took a deep breath before responding.

But Bea went on, "Most of the kids these days are too enthralled with becoming crime scene investigators, or lawyers, or reality TV stars. How many crimes do we have to have to support all of them, and their lawyers? We're going to have a glut of lawyers and investigators, and a dearth of skilled workers who can actually make things work." Bea paused, her frustration deepening.

Haf jumped in first, "We just don't have the money to pump into the retirement fund, and begin a hiring campaign, and sink a lot of money into training. We just don't. You know how weak the economy is Bea. We're struggling to meet our forecast for sales, cash and profits. You know what will happen to our stock price if we miss our quarterly forecast. And you know what will happen to the value of your stock options don't you. What's your point?" Haf didn't mention what would happen to value of *his* stock options.

Bea paused for a moment, "Well, someday I'm hoping to retire too, and I'd like to see my pension plan secure, and I'd like to see the company continue to be successful. If we don't address this, now, we're putting the company at greater risk.

My options aren't nearly as big as yours, so I'm more dependent on the pension plan. Besides, why don't we take the hit now, so that in three to five years, we'll be in much better shape for the future"

Al jumped in, since it looked like the discussion was about to escalate, "The three of us may not be here in five years, if we don't get our house in order. And, if we're too short-sighted, the business may not be here after that." Clearly these were difficult times for Dumberning.

"Bea and Haf, I want you to work together, along with the VP of Operations, to develop three scenarios on this, one where we do nothing, another where we do a half-hearted effort, kind of like we're doing now, and the final one where we address this issue in a comprehensive manner. Play this out over the next 5-10 years. I want this to include the following:

1. Reinvigorating our apprenticeship program to replace say half of those we expect to retire.

2. Working with local trade schools and community colleges to develop programs for providing skilled workers, assume that will provide 25% of the people we need.

3. Re-hiring retirees who want to come back to work on a contract basis; maybe another 25% will come from that.

4. A more intensive internal training program on our processes.

5. Improving our productivity, and particularly our OEE in manufacturing, to determine its effect on these scenarios. If we could go from 50% OEE to 75%, we could take a 6-day three shift operation to a 6-day two

shift operation, and not need to replace nearly as many people. I'd like to know what's realistic here.

I'd like to go to the board with a proposal on our plan of action, and the consequences of all this. I do think we have a crisis in waiting, and we need to address it now, not five years from now. That may be too late. If it affects our share price in the short term, I'm willing to make the case for doing this. We do still need to make sure we can cash flow the business, and keep our balance sheet in order."

The Lesson: The retirement of the baby boomer generation is a crisis in waiting, both from a skilled worker view, and from a social services view. Long term plans are essential to minimize the negative consequences of this.

Epilogue – There are reportedly some 3,000,000 skilled jobs available in an economy with 8% unemployment. Go figure.

To Contract, Or Not To Contract, That Is The Question

13

Wihickey was having a great deal of difficulty. Overall market conditions were flat, but foreign competition was increasing dramatically, and other costs or revenue losses seemed to be increasing, no matter the effort put into reducing them.

"Stuff" seemed to happen routinely to bust the budgets, e.g., an unexpected plant shutdown requiring extraordinary repairs and lost revenue, an accident necessitating considerable management attention and analysis (and additional costs), etc.

And, a new product introduction from a competitor was forcing markdowns on existing Wihickey products. The list seemed to go on.

Beanne Counters, the CFO, believed that there were a lot of opportunities to save money, and be more competitive. Beanne had recently attended a seminar by a famous management consultant who extolled the value of focusing on "core competencies", and contracting out anything which was not core. The logic seemed quite good – let's focus on what we do best in our business, and contract the work we don't do well to others that do, because it is their core competency. They should be more efficient at what they do best, and save us money.

Two areas of particular interest to Beanne were – computer systems and software maintenance, and plant maintenance. These seemed ripe for the picking. After all, he reasoned, anyone with a high school education and a little training could fix a piece of equipment couldn't they? It was just maintenance, something done on his car regularly by a guy with greasy hands. As for computer systems, anyone could load a set of software from a disk and re-boot couldn't they? Why should the company have employees do that when you could get that service much cheaper from a contractor?

Beanne had done some preliminary work on this, having a few contractors come in for talks about what they could do and what it might cost. Scope was not included, but typical rates and responsibilities, and a few references were reviewed. Beanne concluded from these discussions that it would indeed be cheaper to have the contractors do certain work. For example, the fully loaded rate (salaries, benefits and overheads) for the company's computer techs was $70 per hour, whereas the contractor was quoting $60. Similar data was provided from maintenance contractors. Doing a simple calculation, he reckoned the company could save millions per year, given current headcount and rate differentials.

So, with this information in hand, Beanne approached the CEO, Likta Goalong, outlining his proposal.

"Folks in IT and at the plants aren't going to be happy with this," remarked the Likta.

"Yeah, well the geeks in IT don't have a clue about finances and how the company makes money. Save a dollar, make a dollar is what I always say," crowed Beanne.

After a brief pause, he went on, "And, those guys at the plants would break an anvil, just to show how quickly they can fix it," he went on in a caustic tone, "bunch of bozos."

"I wouldn't repeat that when you go for their input", Likta said, with a smirk on his face. Getting back to business, Likta asked, "Are these estimates real, $50 million in reduced costs?"

"Of course they're real," Beanne responded almost sarcastically, as if Likta couldn't see the beauty of his calculations for each business unit. So, after a little more discussion Likta gave his tentative approval for contracting IT and plant maintenance. But he indicated that Beanne would have to get feedback from the VP's of IT and Manufacturing, and report back to him with his final draft plan before actually proceeding.

The next week didn't go as smoothly for Beanne. The VP of IT, Gotta Lottadata, who had just transferred from Italy, didn't really appreciate what Beanne was suggesting, that her people were more expensive than contractors and consultants. She'd seen and approved some of the invoices coming from contractors. She also didn't like the thought of the size of her empire diminishing. She had also heard of others trying this with mixed results, and even horror stories – lost data, nearly missed payrolls, vendors upset over payment delays.

So, Beanne responded, "Tell me how you're going to save us $10 million per year in costs, like I've just outlined with my approach."

"With the current systems, reports, and multiple interfaces on various hardware, I don't think I can," Gotta replied, noting that she inherited the current system design from her predecessor.

Continuing, she said "To maintain current systems and performance at a lower cost would actually require investing another $50 million in new or consolidated equipment and software. We'd get lower costs of $10-15 million per year, but only with such an investment."

"Bullcrap", responded Beanne sharply, "Every time I come here asking you to lower your costs, you always come back by asking for more money. It ain't gonna' happen." Beanne left abruptly, steaming out the door.

After a cool-down period, Beanne decided to go talk to the VP of Operations, Mark Makumquik. This one didn't go very well either.

After listening patiently to Beanne's proposal, Mark responded obliquely "You ever worked in operations?"

"No," Beanne replied firmly, "but I see operations' results every day, and we're spending a lot more money than we did, especially on maintenance. The manufacturing costs are going up 3-5% per year. Seems to me that last year you promised to reduce maintenance costs by 10%, but that's not happening. What's the problem?"

The Mark, feeling a bit defensive, observed that "Production demands increased, necessitating additional maintenance, and we actually delivered higher gross profits than budgeted, in spite of the higher operating costs."

"You're not a profit center, you're a cost center," hissed Beanne, "Can't you manage your costs?" Things went sharply downhill from there, and Beanne was quickly invited to leave Mark's office.

Beanne went back to the Likta and summarized the feedback "They weren't very helpful, and didn't offer any alternatives to what I suggested. All they want to do is keep their little empires intact. We've got to get our costs down if we want to survive market conditions and maintain our balance sheet and terms with the banks."

Reluctantly, after some intense discussions, Likta decided to go along with Beanne and instructed the VP's of IT and Operations to proceed with contracting out major portions of their operations. Bids were let, negotiations ensued, along with selection of the contractors. The contractors finally arrived to "take over" tasks within each operation.

The IT contractors arrived with great enthusiasm, looking forward to being introduced to the folks they were replacing, and to be briefed on the systems, hardware, and software. They were bright, energetic, beaming with pride, well-intentioned, and except for their veteran manager, about as green as their young looks would suggest. Granted, they had been trained in most all the relevant software and hardware in college, and had grown up in the "internet age", many working with computers since they were children. Though Gotta had thought they would be more experienced, like the business people who had sold the job to Wihickey. "Apparently the veterans who sell the work aren't the same people that do the work," she surmised.

Saying the contractors were childishly insensitive and a bit unkempt would be giving them too much credit for having good manners. Of course this only further alienated the existing staff.

The staff were told to explain to the incoming contractors how systems were configured, the process used for configuration and document control, the requirements for system upgrades and maintenance, the current problems in the systems and their status, contacts and key personnel with the various vendors, and the patches into certain systems that weren't fully integrated. The list went on.

You could imagine that the current staff members were less than enthusiastic about the transfer of information to the incoming folks, whose demeanor did not help. They tried to be professional about the transfer, but given their short-timer status, and their soon-to-be lack of having a vested interest in the company's future, the transfer did not go particularly well.

About a week later, Mark called the contractor's IT Manager, Herta Help, with a major problem. The data on inventory and shipments was suddenly unavailable, and one of his biggest plants was updating their monthly production plans. They couldn't do their production planning without this data.

"Where's my inventory and shipment data?" Mark asked urgently.

Herta was surprised, "Oh, the system is down while we track down a problem with one of the patches between accounts receivable, shipments, and inventory. We were told there had been some errors in this, such that the accounts didn't balance and it deserved top priority"

"You think you might have asked me about the best time for doing this?" responded Mark, sounding both desperate and angry at the same time, "We're doing our monthly production planning and quarterly MRP runs."

"This impacts raw material orders, our suppliers, equipment setups and just about everything we do in operations. How soon will you have it back on line?"

"Tomorrow, we hope", answered Herta, sounding somewhat desperate.

"You hope?"

"Yeah, it's a pretty complex system with several patches, none of which are well documented, so we're having to review the code line by line."

The conversation didn't get much better after this, with Herta advising that Beanne had said to get this problem fixed, NOW. And, since he actually reported to Beanne, he felt he should get right on this problem.

Eventually, the problem was resolved, but not before delays in ordering raw material and production planning, the creation of excess inventory in one product line, but having insufficient inventory in another product line, thus delaying shipments to their best customer. That best customer of course was more than a little upset. They had already served notice that if Wihickey had any more delays, they'd have to look to another vendor to make sure their supply chain was fully functional.

Similar problems happened with HR, where payroll was impacted, since HR had the responsibility to provide accounting with all the appropriate information about pay rates, withholding, 401K contributions, and so on. People got paid, but tax withholdings weren't quite right for some employees, 401K contributions were a bit off for some from not having been updated in a timely manner, and other deductions were not quite right for several others.

All this caused a tremendous mess for accounting and HR who had to work through the problems and get them corrected, not to mention the frustration, and loss of productivity, with employees reporting problems reviewing the corrections.

But, Beanne took solace in the fact that they were saving money with the cheaper contractor.

Down in the operating plants a different, yet similar story was unfolding.

The contractor arrived and immediately set to work putting in place new systems (the ones they were familiar with), bringing people up to speed on roles and responsibilities, and setting out task assignments. Indeed, some of the "old hands" from Wihickey went to the contractor after being laid off from the company. This helped quite a bit, but that help was exacerbated by the fact that the contractor had different work management systems (that had to be learned by the old hands), and a different philosophy regarding maintenance.

They knew that they made money through billable hours, so putting in place a system to maximize billable hours, in good conscience of course, was good for their business. And, they had reviewed all the equipment's PM schedules, modifying some based on their experience. Having done this, they rigidly stuck to the PM schedule (it was a key performance indicator with Wihickey), and if needed, worked overtime to cover reactive and emergency maintenance. Life was good, for the contractor.

Beau Weevil, one of the old hands, was assigned to do a PM on a set of equipment to replace the wear plates. "Doing PM and taking care of the equipment is a good thing," thought Beau.

But then he observed out loud to his supervisor, "There's nothing wrong with these wear plates. They aren't worn, loose, or scored." He went on, "Didn't we do an inspection on these just a month ago and they were fine? Why would we spend the money to replace something that's not broken?"

"It's on the PM schedule, and we get a bonus for schedule compliance," advised Dem Witt, his supervisor, "so get your butt out there and do the job you were hired to do."

"But, but, there's nothing wrong with the equipment," protested Beau, stammering just a bit, and not wanting to upset his new boss.

"You're not deaf are you?" Dem said sharply.

So, Beau apologized, and went on about the job. Unfortunately, the operations people didn't give him enough time to do the job properly. So, rather than check the plate's dimensions and precision, he assumed they were (even though they'd been in stores for a long time), and he didn't have time to use some of the tools for a precision installation, simply banging the old ones off and the new ones on.

Sadly, those same plates failed abruptly about a month later, in the middle of the night, and guess who got the call to come fix them? Beau of course – his name was on the work order for the PM. And, speaking rhetorically, guess who didn't get enough time to do the job properly this time either? Beau complained loudly, only to be told to shut up and get the machine back on line. They had already lost 4 hours of production, likely 6-8 now, and this was likely to impact a critical delivery to a key customer.

"See you in another month," Beau told the shift supervisor as he left. Beau knew that the wear plates, properly installed, should last at least a year, not weeks or months. He also knew that a simple inspection would tell you when you should replace them, and not just do it on a time basis. But, his was a lone voice in the new wilderness, and he was just glad to have a job.

Interestingly, as the contractor did more PM (time/calendar-based maintenance), reactive and emergency maintenance also increased. Spare parts consumption (and costs) also increased proportionally. Whereas before, the plant had been doing much of its maintenance based on the condition of the equipment, they were now doing much more of it based on calendar time. And costs were increasing. No one seemed to understand that the greatest risk of failure was during the infant mortality period shortly after startup. Incredibly, maintenance costs doubled in the first quarter after the arrival of the contractor, and production output dropped, since they were taking the equipment down more often to do the PM, and in fact were experiencing more unplanned downtime due to abrupt failures.

But, Beanne took solace in the fact that they were saving money with the contractors who charged at a lower rate, thinking to himself, "Imagine how much all this would have cost if they had the old staff in place."

In the meantime, uptime went down, downtime went up, costs went up, particularly in maintenance, and on time delivery suffered. So much for saving money by contracting.

The Lessons: 1) Replacing one set of warm bodies with another will not provide better results if your processes are broken. 2) Contractors are intended to supplement your workforce, not supplant them.

Epilogue –

Most companies need contractors, and indeed, contractors are typically an integral part of any organization, e.g., for high skill, low-frequency tasks (e.g., turbine generator balancing), for low skill, high-frequency tasks (e.g., custodial), for one time startup/shutdown tasks.

Toyota's model is to get the processes working really well before contracting them. That way the processes are understood well enough to manage them effectively.

Leadership - Rank Is Not the Same as Expertise

14

We enter the scene with of a major capital project at Karainjini Corporation, one under intense pressure to get a new plant started up and on line, making product. It's already 6 months late, and $50 million over budget. The project manager is, as they say, "beside himself".

"Why can't we start up unit 1 today?" demanded Cal Kulaten, the project manager. The intense pressure was evident.

"Well, we can start the run-up process today, but doing it properly will take about 48 hours. It has a very slow ramp up to minimize the risk of inducing excess thermal stress on the equipment, and to minimize the risk of chemical fouling because of inadequate oxidation in the process. The process is new and we have no data on how it will perform as we ramp up," responded Kim Icaltek, a chemical engineer, and Cal's chief process engineer for the project.

"New, what do you mean new? We did trials on the prototype for this, and had it up and running in 12 hours," retorted Cal, clearly frustrated at yet another delay in startup.

"The problem is that the process may, or may not, scale up according to the prototype data. Right now we just don't know. Some indications are that we can, but other data suggests we can't. We just don't know," Kim said, with a tone of concern, even fear, in her voice, as she pointed to some charts on fouling factors and rates, along with yields and efficiencies.

Cal's eyes glazed over. He wasn't a chemical engineer, and had little interest in those issues. He was a civil engineer. He built plants and got them started, and this one was getting to be a huge blot on his career, which up to now had been stellar (at least in his own eyes).

Finally, after staring mindlessly at the charts for a few seconds, he demanded "What can we do to get this thing up and running by tomorrow morning. I promised corporate that we'd be into our first production run at the latest by tomorrow. They even called this morning to ask if we were on line yet."

"Who's they?" asked Kim

"My boss," replied Cal dismissively, "Who else? And he's getting a lot of pressure from his boss, the CEO. Poop flows downhill. Haven't you heard?" The sarcasm was in full bloom. Incidentally, the CEO had promised certain investors that production would begin tomorrow.

Kim was now trying to maintain her composure, and it was difficult. Everyone had been under extreme pressure for several months, and it was intensifying with each day. Kim was also the resident expert on this type of system and had a better understanding of it than anyone on site.

"If we try to ramp up too quickly, we'll be taking all kinds of risks. Not just the relatively small risks like excess fouling, but more severe risks, like a cracked exchanger and reactor vessel, even an explosion. This is a really volatile process, and it has to be treated with extreme care," pleaded Kim.

Ignoring her pleading, Cal ordered, "I want this thing up and running by tomorrow noon. Is that clear?" He was intent on making good on his latest promise. His career just couldn't afford another missed deadline.

Kim sat, looking at the floor, and ignoring her boss for the moment. Finally, she took a deep breath and looked Cal in the eyes, firmly asking, "Are you ordering me to start up at a faster rate than I think is reasonable, recognizing the risks?" After she asked this, she looked around the room and took note of who was present.

"Yes, damn it, I am. Just be careful as you do it," Cal replied as he walked away, "I've got another meeting now." He couldn't get out of the room fast enough.

Kim sat and thought for a moment, and then began giving instructions to the operators on what to do and what to look for. As the day wore on, the process seemed to be ramping up relatively smoothly. They were increasing the flow rate and pressure above the prototype trials to accelerate the startup, but the system seemed to be handling it well.

Kim was just about to take a break and go get some sleep, after giving the operators some final instructions, when she, and everyone else in the control room, heard a low, dull "whomp". They all looked at each other with puzzled expressions.

"What was that?" Kim asked to no one in particular.

The operators began looking at the various parameters on the control panels, searching for any problems that might be indicated. "We've had a slight pressure pulse on the unit. But, it seems to be back into the normal range. A bit low though," one of the operators said, pointing to the screen.

Kim looked around and spotted Hicks Boson, one of the operating supervisors, a small guy, but one with huge influence in the plant. "Hicks, would you take a walk around the unit and see if there's anything unusual?" Hicks grabbed his hardhat and left.

"Anything else showing up?" she asked. Heads shook in the negative direction.

Moments later, Hicks came back in, hurrying. "We've got a slight leak on the heat exchanger. Looks like we've popped a gasket," reported Hicks, "It's on the shell side, so it's probably ok. No hazardous material in the shell."

"Any indication of any leaks on the tube side?" Kim asked.

Hicks looked at the panel, and said "No, but flow seems to be on a slightly downward trend, and pressure seems to be decreasing some."

"We'd better start to reduce the rate," Kim instructed, "The systems doesn't seem to be doing very well on this accelerated startup."

Just as she said this, there was another similar, but different "whomp" and then a kind of "ping".

"Now," Kim ordered, becoming increasingly alarmed.

"Hicks, go have another look," Kim said urgently, and immediately went to the control panel to instruct the operators on an emergency shutdown.

As they were in the middle of shutting down, Hicks came running back in, nearly shouting.

"The heat exchanger leak is worse now, and something else seems to be going on. We may have breached the tube side. It's making a funny noise, and heat exchangers don't normally do that."

Kim seemed to listen to Hicks intently, and ignore him at the same time. She was focused on watching and guiding the emergency shutdown process.

After considerable angst and effort, the system was finally shutdown.

After everything had stabilized, Kim called Cal at midnight to report on the incident. Needless to say, Cal was not happy.

"I told you to be careful when you started up," Cal howled.

"Yes, and you also ordered me to accelerate the startup process, and get it on line by tomorrow noon. That's an 18 hour startup period versus the 48 hours I specifically recommended," Kim responded sharply.

"Did not," Cal responded, almost childishly, "I asked you if you could." The finger pointing had already started.

Not wanting to get into a long argument with Cal, Kim interrupted, "Look, we've got a lot of work to do here. I've already got an emergency maintenance crew here to take the heat exchanger apart to determine the nature of the problems and to try to get it back on line. I'll get back to you. By the way, we don't have a spare heat exchanger." She hung up, much to Cal's chagrin.

Hours passed, and eventually went into days. The heat exchanger was a total wreck, and they had no spare.

The increased temperature and thermal transient induced by the rapid startup had reduced the mechanical strength of the heat exchanger tube bundle. The increased rate of fouling induced by the increased flow and rate of startup had increased the weight inside the tube bundle, adding additional stress. When combined with the increased pressures on startup, some of the tubes in the tube bundle began to fail. As the weight of the tube bundle began to increase from the fouling, it began to put pressure on the shell and the flanged fittings.

It also turned out that the wrong gasket was used for the flanges, and were not torqued properly, causing a leak on the shell side. This wasn't helped by the fact that the entire shell was under extra torsion because the bolt holes didn't align very well at installation, and the piping had been twisted to align the bolt holes for attaching the flange face. And, to top it all off, the foundation was weaker than it should have been to hold the entire fixture in place.

The project was delayed another month, as the repairs were made and the plant was reviewed for other similar potential problems. Eventually it did get on line, but not before severely damaging Cal's reputation. Kim didn't escape unscathed, since she had gone ahead with the startup, knowing the serious risks that were being taken. But, she did have her witnesses that Cal had ordered her to startup, carefully. It's hard to be careful in a situation fraught with danger.

The Lesson: Rank is not the same as expertise. Real leaders will rely on the expertise of others in making the decisions that come with the leader's rank.

Align the Organization Using Performance Measures 15

Joseph Juran famously said "If you don't measure it, you don't manage it." While I agree, it's also important that your measures help an organization to work in concert, not conflict. The model of using management by objectives, or MBO, while seemingly a good model, too often encourages people to work in conflict, that is, achieving their individual objectives, to the detriment of the organization's overall objectives.

Ivada Nuff stared blankly into the air. It was time for developing the annual business plan, and as usual, a part of this would be coming up with performance measures that would determine a big part of his income, consisting of his base pay, plus a bonus based on performance. It was an annual ritual at Mungaroona Company, one that he very much disliked, much the same as getting, or giving, performance appraisals.

His biggest worry was that he didn't control many of the variables that affected his performance. He had historically been held accountable for costs, but his costs were mostly influenced by the actions of others. If operations didn't operate the equipment properly, or hadn't been trained to do so, that would induce a lot of repairs, which came from his budget, not theirs. He didn't control the operating practices, or the training program. His scheduling for the routine work of doing preventive and planned corrective maintenance was also at the whim of the operating supervisors. They would often delay or cancel the planned work, inducing lots of inefficiencies in the work.

Even when he was able to work to the schedule, the spare parts were sometimes not available to actually do the work. And, unplanned downtime was almost always because of some problem with the design or operation of the equipment. Yet, all these were typically his performance measures. He was really frustrated with this.

Over in the store room, there was a similar situation, and Sper Pertz, the store room manager, had similar angst. He was being pressured to reduce the inventory level of spares by his boss in procurement, but too often would not have the spare parts that maintenance requested, resulting in a so-called stockout. He wasn't criticized by his boss for stockouts, but he was for keeping too much inventory. He just didn't enjoy the criticism from Ivada when the stockout occurred. He really wanted to do a good job for Ivada, but felt constrained in his ability to do that.

In Purchasing, Per Kurmint, the senior manager, was intently focused on his key performance measures, which made up a large chunk of his annual pay. His measures were related to reducing the costs for raw material and equipment supply, and reducing the inventory levels of raw material and spare parts. Excess inventory was working capital that wasn't working. Per published monthly reports on how much his department had saved, and how inventory was being reduced. Per reported to the CFO, Fen Ancier.

Meanwhile, over in the marketing and sales department, Sal Degudstuf, was lamenting the company's quality and on time delivery performance. He wasn't accountable for this, but it affected his sales. His objective was bookings and market share for the products. He wasn't held accountable for unit cost, or gross profit, or on time delivery, or quality either. That was the site manager and his production manager.

Sal would, however, often call the site and insist on changing the production schedule to give priority to different orders than had been agreed the previous week or month. He had yet another "hot one", and each one seemed to hold the future of the company in balance. Of course, this would disrupt the production schedule and have other knock-on effects, but that wasn't his worry.

A short while later, a planning meeting to review next year's budgets was held corporate headquarters, including setting performance goals and measures. The CEO, Ima Deboss, met with each site manager and their staff to finalize the plans, and included Sal, Per, and Fen, among others, in the meetings. Ima wanted to make sure he understood each site's plans and how it fit into supporting the overall business goals, and how his staff could be more effective in that effort.

Ima began, "Let's look at our performance measures in each of the departments to make sure we've set the right goals. Dee, give us a quick brief on your overall site objectives."

Dee Fensiv, the site manager, began "Well, as you know, we're under intense pressure for cost reduction on our products, all the while improving our quality and delivery performance. So, my plan includes a 5% reduction in total unit cost, a 5% improvement in on time delivery to 95%, a reduction in scrap/waste from 3% to 2%, and a 30% reduction in returns, complaints, and credits. But, we've got several problems, one with raw material quality, another with disruptions to our production plans, and another with inventory levels." Dee glanced at his production manager, Pam Demonium, "These problems are driving Pam crazy."

Sal, Per and Fen all perked up with the last comment.

Dee continued, "Yes, the raw material is cheaper, but the yields are really quite poor because of its quality, and it's harder to process. We have considerable re-work on some of the products, and it looks like we're going to have more scrap. All this makes it harder to achieve some of my objectives."

"Wait a minute," interjected Per, "Don't start blaming me for problems with your operation. I've worked my butt off to get better prices for everything we buy. We've save $100M this year on that alone." Per wanted Ima to know how good he was at lowering costs.

"Well, we may not save anything, if my yields and scrap go to hell in a hand basket," Dee responded, just a bit sarcastically.

Ima held his hand up, looking at Per and Fen, "Go on... finish, and then we'll have the debate."

Dee continued, "As for on time delivery, we have nearly daily interruptions from sales wanting to change our production schedules. We want to be responsive to Sal and the customer, but these constant interruptions and changeovers sure play havoc with our production plans, and our delivery performance. It doesn't help quality or scrap either, having to make so many changes."

Now it was Sal's be defensive, "So, it my fault you can't deliver on time? What about that big shutdown you had last month that delayed a quarter of our deliveries? Was that my fault?"

"No, we didn't have the parts we needed on site, and had to have them air freighted to get us back on line. Sper told me we weren't holding those parts here anymore, said Per was cutting back on inventory," Dee responded.

Dee was beginning to get agitated, much like everyone else in the room. When you get into people's bonus structure they get really sensitive.

Now Per jumped back in, "So, this one is my fault as well. Boy you sure have a way of blaming everybody else for your performance." Per's face was red now, not to mention his temperament.

Ima injected himself again, "Everyone take a deep breath. We're going to listen first, then we're going to have a rational debate, not a fight." As he said this he looked around the room making eye contact with each person.

Dee finished with "Inventory, particularly in spares, but also in raw material. There have been times when we had to change our production schedules because of a lack of raw material for a given product. We're doing this just-in-time thing now to lower our inventories, and reduce our working capital, but our suppliers aren't particularly reliable about their deliveries, or their quality. And, well, I just mentioned the spares problem we had last month with that breakdown. I'm all for reducing our working capital, but it's really having an impact on our production."

Now Fen jumped in, "So, Dee, your plant breaks down, and it's my or Per's fault that you don't have the spares? What are you doing to make sure you don't break down? And another thing, your maintenance costs are exorbitant? What's with that? If you don't get your maintenance costs down, I'll get them down for you." Tensions were high at this point.

Ima interjected himself again, looking at Dee, and then Ivada, but addressing Ivada,

"What about this Ivada, what are you doing to reduce your maintenance costs and downtime? The benchmarking we just had done says we're way out of line."

Actually, they were just slightly above average for their industry, but Ima was trying to make a point, and rattled off the data.

A lump went into Ivada's throat. He thought he was just going to be a bystander and listen during this meeting. He couldn't imagine the CEO would know the details of his maintenance costs.

He took a deep breath and began, hesitantly, stammering just a bit, and not reflecting much confidence, "Well, Mr. Deboss, the main problem with my maintenance costs is that I don't control most of the variables that affect those costs. Our biggest cost is related to repairs. We just did several root cause analyses on the equipment failures, including that one we had last month, and most of the failures were because we don't have good operating practices – startup, shutdown, and general operation. But, I don't think that's because of poor operators. A lot of it is because we haven't trained them effectively, or the procedures aren't definitive enough.

We've had several problems related to design, and I have to admit our maintenance practices are not very good. We're working on both those. And, a lot of times my plans for maintenance get delayed, either because of a breakdown, or because of a change in the production plan," looking at Sal when he said this, "This induces a lot of inefficiency in the work. We've already mentioned the lack of spares being readily available, which causes delays too. All this has a huge impact on our production and financial performance." Ivada wasn't very high in the organization, but he clearly understood many of the issues affecting their performance.

Everyone sat in stunned silence, searching for their defensive position.

Thereupon a lively debate ensued and there was much "gnashing of the teeth." Through it all, Ima inserted himself as coach and referee, but demanding that people begin to think about the consequences of their performance and measures on each other, and on the overall goals of the organization.

Finally, Ima held his hand up, "OK, I've heard enough. I want to give all this some thought. Let's continue this meeting tomorrow morning. I'll postpone the other meetings I have tomorrow. This is important enough, and your ideas good enough that I want to use this as a model for the other plants. We've got to get better alignment in the organization, and better performance measures to facilitate that alignment. We can't be working at cross-purposes to achieve individual goals to the overall detriment of the business."

That evening Ima gave a lot of thought to the discussions during the day.

The next day, he began the meeting with "I've given considerable thought to our discussion and I'm proposing the following measures be used to make sure we work together:

1. Sal, I'm going to hold you accountable for the usual bookings and market share numbers in each product line, but I'm also holding you accountable for production plan disruptions, and gross profit per unit of product. I recognize the some disruptions may be essential, but those should be minimized. I want to think about having on-time-delivery be one of yours, but for the time being that's on hold.

2. Fen, I'm going to hold you accountable for cash flow, payables, receivables, inventory levels, as usual, but for you and Per I'm adding stockout rate, and particularly its impact on production and delivery because of the unavailability of spare parts. I'm also going to hold you accountable for that portion of our scrap and yield that relates to raw material. On the spares inventory, or on our raw material purchases, we can't be robbing Peter to pay Paul.

3. Dee, of course you and Pam are going to be held accountable for unit cost, gross profit per unit, on-time-delivery, and quality, but I'm adding a couple to Pam's. Pam is going to be held accountable for maintenance and repair costs, unplanned downtime, and for maintenance schedule compliance – the production plan must include the maintenance plan. We can't expect two separate plans for work effectively. Ivada makes a good case that most of these losses are coming from poor operating practices, so I want that to be part of your thinking. I'll make more money available for training operators.

4. Ivada, I'm going to hold you accountable for those same performance measures, but I'm adding a few – on-time-delivery – I don't want you to insist on doing maintenance when a critical delivery is at risk; and stockout rate and inventory turns on spares. Per, you'll also have stockout rate and inventory turns. I want you and Ivada to work together to get the balance right. The ideal state is minimal stock and minimal stockouts, both. You'll not likely ever get it perfect, but you'll do a damn site better than what you're doing right now.

5. We're all going to be held accountable for safety. I've seen considerable data that indicates the more reactive we are, the higher the risk of injury, and the higher our costs, because work is being done in an uncontrolled manner. We've got to get this right.

The management team proceeded with implementing the measures that Ima had made clear he wanted. At first there was some grumbling and irritation with one another, but as time passed, and as Ima continued to make clear that this was essential, the managers began to work more closely together.

In time performance improved, dramatically, and everyone began to see the value of having cross-functional measures to help assure a balanced approach. They were much more closely aligned to the overall business purpose.

The Lessons: 1) Performance measures must be balanced, and must assure that people work in concert, not conflict. 2) Measures must optimize the system, not the silo.

What Would Mom Say? A Story of Ethics

"Look what we've got," Dee Septive exclaimed! Phil
Harmonic, the president of Toolonga, stared at the package,
with the proverbial "deer in the headlights" look.

"What?" he quizzed, still puzzled by the package sitting in
front of him.

"Ann O'Nimity, our sales manager on the west coast, went
dumpster diving near Ramol, and found this," Dee continued
excitedly. Ramol was the company's biggest, most intense
competitor.

"Found what," Phil replied, in a more annoyed tone.

"Just look," Dee pointed to the stack of paper and drawings
on the table as he spread them out.

Phil suddenly noticed Ramol's logo on some of the papers, as
it slowly began to dawn on him what he was looking at.

"Look, this is a drawing of their newest instrument in the
Lamda line. You know, the one that competes with our
flagship Alpha line," Dee went on, "And, look at this, it's their
spec sheet, and this, their schematics for the instrument.
There's even more – here's an outline of their marketing
plan."

Phil suddenly had a sickening feeling surging throughout his body. "What have we done?" he was thinking, knowing at the same time, what had been done. "Who has seen this?" he demanded of Dee, showing his frustration with the whole situation.

"Well, just Ann and me. I thought you'd want to see it first," he said, sensing Phil's irritation, but not noticing that he would obviously be the third to see it, not the first.

Phil was feeling a bit lightheaded about the whole situation. He had said many times "What we do here must stand up in the light of day." He didn't think this would pass that test. His mind was going through any number of thoughts, manic might even describe his thinking.

After what seemed like a very long time, but couldn't have been more than a few seconds, he ordered, "I do NOT want to see this, and I don't want you or Ann to look at it again. I want to talk with our attorney about the implications of this. Put this in a safe place where no one but you has access. And, do not make any copies of any of this."

Phil quickly got on the phone to the company attorney, Bill Hours, and briefed him on the situation, asking for his guidance. Bill, as attorneys are want to do, pontificated about the ramifications of the documents, how they had been obtained, where they were, who had seen them, and how they might be used, among other things. To sum up his answer, having them may or may not be illegal, depending on exactly where and how they were obtained, and what the statutes in that state say about this type of action and situation. He asked if Phil would like him to look into this further.

In the middle of the lecture, Phil finally interrupted and said abruptly "No thanks, I'll handle it. Look, whether these documents were obtained legally or illegally, having them is unethical. I would rather people not know we have them, and we will not use them. I intend to have the documents destroyed, without reviewing them, but want you to be prepared to help us if the issue goes any further than this."

He hung up, and quickly called Dee, "Where's Ann today?" Dee replied hesitantly, "Oh, she's here for a meeting. She brought those files with her, and…"

Phil interrupted "Drop whatever you're doing and come to my office, now, with Ann!" There was little patience in his voice.

"But, we're in the middle of a meeting," objected Dee.

"I don't care. We're going resolve this issue of having Ramol's documents, and we're going to do it today," Phil asserted.

Five minutes later they arrived, obviously irritated at having their other meeting interrupted. Phil held his hand up before either could say anything.

"I've been on the phone to our attorney, and he's advised me that what we've done could be illegal, depending on any number of issues around their acquisition. It could even be a felony." Ann started to talk, but Phil held out his hand in an obvious gesture that he wanted Ann's silence.

"Whether it was legal or illegal, whether we're criminally or tortuously libel, I don't want to debate. What we did was unethical, just plain wrong. Would you want this on the six o'clock news?" he asked as he stared at both of them.

He continued, "What would your mother say if she knew you'd done this?" Both Dee and Ann cracked a tiny smile.

Phil interrupted the smile with a stern comment "This isn't cute or funny. I'm dead serious. What would your mother say?"

Sheepishly Ann responded with "She wouldn't like it. She'd probably say something like 'Didn't I teach you better than to do something like that?'" Dee was nodding in agreement.

Phil continued, "Would you want this on the 6 o'clock news?"

"No," Ann responded quickly.

Phil continued, "I want these documents destroyed, NOW. Postpone your meeting, and take the documents to our shredder, or bring the shredder into a private office – you can use mine if necessary, and destroy them. And, don't do anything like this again. If it happens again, you'll both be fired. And, you're not to discuss this with ANYONE. Am I clear? What we do here must stand up in the light of day. Report back to me when all this is done."

Later that afternoon, Dee and Ann reported back that the documents had been destroyed, much to Phil's relief.

The Lesson: Most ethical issues aren't difficult. Just ask "What would Mom say?" or "Would I want this on the 6 o'clock news?" Then act accordingly.

Part II

Related to Reliability and Operational Excellence

Reliability and Safety – We Believe in Safety, Don't We?

Dewey Workem and his good friend, Naria Minit were in the middle of a safety meeting at Justmiluk Corporation, when the maintenance manager, Fixet Fast, came abruptly into the room, pointing to Dewey and motioning for him to come to the back.

"Dewey, we've got a big problem on the Framastand again. I need you and Naria to get over there and take care of it. It's got the whole place ready to shut down," Fixet exclaimed.

"But boss, we in the middle of learning about the changes to the Lockout/Tagout procedure. You know how important that is to safety. I need to stay til this is done," objected Dewey.

"No, you need to get the Framastand back on line, now. The whole plant is about to shut down because of it," demanded Fixet, "There'll be another class."

"Yeah? When? This is the first one on this in six months," countered Dewey.

"Just get over there," Fixet was growing increasingly impatient.

Dewey relented, motioning to Naria to come with him.

When they arrived, the Framastand machine was in fact down, and a couple of mechanics, Jimmy Knolittle and Jerry Dolittle, were standing there staring at it. They had very little, if any, experience in working on the machine.

Dewey looked at Jerry and asked "Is it de-energized and locked out and tagged out?" before doing anything with the machine.

"Yeah, we just did that, but we're kinda stuck," responded Jerry, living up to his name.

"Yeah, we didn't really know what to do next," added Jimmy, living up to his name as well. Collectively, they were sometimes referred to as "the Little Boys."

Dewey and Naria set to work, finding several problems with the hydraulics and pressure cylinders, and noting a gear box oil leak, when suddenly there was a bright flash and loud "Bam!" startling everyone, and knocking Naria on his butt. Naria sat on the floor with a dazed look on his face.

"What the hell?" Dewey thought aloud, as he got to Naria. "You OK?" he asked quickly.

Naria nodded slowly. "I think so... I was just disconnecting the power to the driver... and now I'm sitting on the floor," he responded deliberately, hesitantly. His mouth was slightly open, his eyes trance-like.

Dewey quickly looked Naria over, but only found a bad burn at the tip of his fingers. He instructed Jimmy and Jerry to get the medical people here right away, but they were already on it. At least in this case they knew what to do, and did it quickly.

After a fairly intensive investigation, it turned out that the Framastand had been re-wired by the engineer a few days prior to its latest breakdown, turning a single power circuit into two circuits. The engineer had decided that one of the problems with the machine, among many, was overloading of the power circuit under certain operating conditions, causing it to trip. Since the machine was critical to production he did an on-the-spot modification, and planned to revise the circuit drawings a few days later. He told the maintenance and production supervisors on shift about the change.

Unfortunately, this was not relayed to Dewey, Naria, or Jerry or Jimmy, or others. One reason was that they had been off during that period, and another reason was that the shift supervisors weren't on when they were. So, the circuit that Jerry and Jimmy knew about had been isolated, since they had done it several times before, but not the new circuit to one of the drivers.

The leader of the investigation, Luke Intuit, observed in his analysis:

1. This was the fifth significant failure of the Framastand in the past month, three of which resulted in injuries, two very minor, but the most recent one being the most serious, and potentially deadly. The equipment history indicated a series of problems over the past year, which had intensified in the past month.
2. Of the five recent failures, one was a design problem – indeed with the electrical circuitry; three were operating problems – operating the system beyond its inherent capability (in a rush for production), and tripping it out; and the fifth was a maintenance problem – failing to change the extremely dirty hydraulic fluid causing very rapid wear and failure. The operating and maintenance problems could be

traced to pressures on production, and costs – running the system beyond its capability in order to "catch up" with production losses; and not taking enough time to filter and/or change the hydraulic fluid.

3. Had Dewey and Naria completed their attendance of the "Lock-out/Tag-out" training, the accident would have been avoided, since the design change to the Framastand was being covered in the training that morning.

Luke observed laconically, "If you do things wrong, the wrong things will happen, but if you do things right, the right things will happen."

He continued, "All these failures increased our exposure to the risk of injury, and of course we saw more injuries. We've got to get our practices right to stop these failures… and costs … and injuries." He then showed a series of data from various facilities that supported his position, adding considerable weight to his pronouncement.

Following this near death experience, they made substantial changes in their practices, and went on to improve substantially in all areas of performance.

The Lessons: 1) Poor reliability increases the risk of injury and costs. Don't wait for a near death experience to prompt you to get your practices right. 2) A reliable plant is a safe plant is a cost effective plant.

Lowest Installed Cost, or Lowest Life Cycle Cost?

Wollongong Corporation wanted to improve its processing of certain materials significantly above its current performance. So, its engineers began working on various options for designing and installing just such a system. They also contacted various engineering and building contractors outlining their preliminary expectations and seeking proposals from them on how this might be accomplished.

After considerable thought, Wollongong concluded that their design specs could be met by Duzit & Well, and maybe a couple others. Perhaps as importantly, they also concluded they didn't have the design and project expertise inside the company to take on such a large effort. They would manage the effort by the project engineering firm.

The project was code-named Fleecer, and consisted of a complex mixture of fixed and moving mechanical equipment, along with extensive instrumentation and software to control the entire process. After developing a more detailed specification and putting it out for proposals, Wollongong received a number of bids for the system, and ultimately concluded that Duzit & Well was indeed best qualified and would be the one with whom to negotiate. Unfortunately, Duzit & Well's initial bid was $100M. Richard Cranium, the project manager for Wollongong, was quite put off by the size of the bid, especially since the preliminary estimates had been in the $80M range, and he'd based his entire budget for the project, and to a large measure, his reputation, on the preliminary estimate. He did not want to go back to the board for an extra $20M+, a hugeRichard embarrassment for him.

So, Richard negotiated with Duzit & Well project manager, Dudley Ambler, "Why is your bid now $100M? That's $20M more than the preliminary estimates," he demanded.

Dudley patiently went through a long list of issues, "Well Giter, here on page 21 of your spec you indicate that you need run-rates of 100 parts per minute, but in the final spec you're showing 120 parts per minute. That puts a lot of additional stress on the equipment, so we had to upgrade the motors and drives, the rolls, add hardening material to certain areas with higher wear rates, and modify the software to accommodate the higher speeds, set points, alarms, and so on."

Richard was not sympathetic, drolling out "Well you said the system could do up to 120 parts per minute, and that's what I want."

"Yes Richard, Dudley said, "we said *up to* 120 per minute", emphasizing the words "up to". "That rate is in short spurts, not on a sustained basis," he went on.

"Well," Richard objected, "that's the rate we now need to make this project viable. If you can't do it, we'll find someone else who can. Besides you told me the max rate of this system was 120, and I used that in my calculations for the business case and return on investment, and even in discussions with the board."

It's interesting that Richard failed to mention this was a maximum rate to anyone else outside the project, seeing it as an engineering triviality. And, Richard knew that he had told the board $90M, but he figured if he could save $10M he would be a hero before the board.

Objecting, Dudley of Duzit, replied, "Yes, I just said we told you that was the max rate for short durations, not the sustained rate. See here in this column, it explains sustained rate and max rate, and how that impacts the equipment." He pointed to their original spec sheet given to Richard early on.

No to be swayed, Richard, being a bit of a bully anyway, increased the decibels in his voice, "I want what I want, and what I want is the system you promised – 120 parts per minute for $80M."

"Look," responded Dudley, "we can give you a system for $80M that can do 120 parts per minute, but it won't be able to sustain that rate for months or even years, at least not without much more frequent maintenance, downtime, and replacement parts.

Richard said firmly, "That's what I want, a system for $80M that can do 120 per minute. Get me that, and you've got the job. Otherwise, we're going to someone else."

Richard was actually bluffing at that point. No one else in his estimation could actually do what was being asked. But, he'd made his career bluffing and gambling on issues like this, and it had worked really well so far. He was viewed as a "can-do" kind of guy.

Anyway, in the back of his mind (or maybe the front), he also knew all that work for maintenance and parts would fall on the maintenance department, and the downtime, well that would be the operations department's problem. He wasn't responsible for those problems. He was determined to save that $20M.

Dudley, not wanting to lose the order, caved to Richard's demands, but also went back and changed the specs on the motors, drives, high wear points, software, and anything else that needed changing, and submitted a bid for $80M. Duzit & Well got the job, with Dudley as project lead. Now comes the hard part.

Duzit & Well, led by Dudley, proceeded to work with Wollongong to get the final design completed and installed, all the while with Richard hovering over Dudley, demanding that he do as much work as possible and minimize the impact on Richard's staff.

One of his engineers, Pferd Nerdley, protested, "But, we need to be there when they're installing equipment to make sure it gets done right."

"How much will that cost?" Richard said, threateningly, "Will you keep to your budget on travel and labor?"

"Do I have a budget?" retorted, Nerdley "I thought you kept a pretty tight reins on those things."

"I do," said Richard, "That's why you're not going just yet. You can wait until we do the final startup test."

"But won't that be a little late?" questioned Pferd, sensing danger ahead.

"Not if they do the job right," hissed Richard, "and if they don't, it'll be up to them to fix it." These kinds of conversations went on, and on, with Richard and his staff taking an arms-length, hands-off approach to monitoring and working with Duzit & Well. Richard was treating it as a turn-key job, something he fully expected.

Well, the day (of reckoning) finally arrived for the initial startup and testing of the system. After the preliminary checks, the vendor slowly started the system, ramping up in steps of 10 units per minute, finally reaching 120 per minute, and for nearly 24 hours everything was just hunkey-dorey.

Suddenly the system crashed. After some investigation, it was determined that one of the motors had overheated, tripping the entire system. Richard was furious.

"You told me the system could do 120 parts per minute." Richard yelled.

"Yes, we did, and it can, for short durations of 1-2 hours. We also told you that too. Look at your spec" fumed the Dudley.

Undeterred, Richard demanded they get the system back on line. Equally undeterred, Dudley said that wouldn't be a problem, but the spare motor would have to be used.

An argument ensued about who would replace the spare motor, which was a very high-speed, and expensive, motor. Ultimately they agreed to disagree and save the debate for the negotiation of the final payment – Duzit & Well had been receiving progress payments, but $5M was being withheld pending final acceptance.

These kinds of problems went on, and on, for months – hardware problems, software and control systems problems. Each time Dudley would pull out the specs and assert having met the spec, and each time Richard would challenge those conclusions.

Finally, Richard dismissed Duzit & Well, threatening to sue for breach of contract (more bluffing, since it had always worked before) and ordered his engineers to work with the operations department to get the system functioning properly. Richard hid his engineering costs under his annual development budget, and demanded that the operating people pony up for the maintenance and parts. While complaining, they had little choice but to go along with Richard's demands – they had previously begun decommissioning other equipment in anticipation of using the new system. It would be expensive to re-start the decommissioned gear.

Meanwhile, in Richard's reports to the board, everything was going fine. Yes, they were having a few teething problems with the new system, but this was normal for a system this complex, and besides, reported Richard, they fully expected to come in under budget by some $10M.

Richard wasn't counting all the time and money being spent by Pferd Nerdley and the other engineers to re-design and make corrections to the system. Nor was he counting all the parts and maintenance costs and production losses due to the downtime being incurred in the operation. Nor was he counting the lost production because the system couldn't sustain 120 units per minute. Richard reported the project complete after three months of startup effort and closed out the accounts, finally relenting on his threats to sue, and paying Duzit & Well most of the money held in retention. A year later, the system was actually doing what it was originally reported to be capable of doing, but this was only after replacing major motors, drives, and other systems out of the operating budgets, along with all the additional spares and training that goes with the changes. They spent another $20M out of pocket, and incurred another $20M in lost production because of all the problems.

At the end of the project Richard got a big promotion and bonus for doing such a great job, having saved some $10M on the project costs approved by the board.

The Lessons: 1) Beware of those who do a better job managing their career than managing the work. 2) Life cycle costs must be considered in any project, including operating, maintenance, lost production, energy, and disposal costs. 3) Managers are often rewarded for short term results, at the risk of long term failure.

Buying the Cheapest Isn't Always the Cheapest

3

As with all companies, Warangi Corporation, was always looking for ways to lower costs, improve quality, and increase market share. Among other initiatives, they were reviewing supply chain management principles.

Penny Pincher, their VP of Procurement, had recently attended a series of seminars on supply chain management, and concluded they could save several hundred million dollars in procurement costs by applying these principles.

So Warangi launched an initiative for reducing its purchasing costs. They consolidated suppliers, moving to a global supplier for each major procurement activity – key raw materials, contractors, equipment, parts and so on.

This consolidation effort was quite the good thing Penny observed. They could now squeeze each of the vendors on price because of the higher volume and reduced marketing costs that each would incur. And, they'd have more leverage over that supplier. What a great position to be in. The only problem with that logic was that you were now beholden to that supplier, so they had better be good, and they had better make enough money to sustain and grow their business as well.

And, they were off, sailing through vendors like a powerful laxative, consolidating, squeezing, cajoling, and demanding. And, things were looking up. They were saving money, lots of money.

Indeed, since they had fewer suppliers, they needed fewer purchasing agents, so many of those were let go. In fact, Penny reported to the executive committee that Warangi had saved some $300M in lower purchasing costs. She had a huge spread sheet listing all the things they bought, along with the each's volume, and each's old price and new price to clearly demonstrate the savings. And Penny was rewarded with a handsome bonus for the effort.

Meanwhile, down in the operations, things weren't so rosy. Aggie Tatid, one of the operators, went to the storeroom looking for some simple materials to do some TLC work on his machinery – tighten, lubricate, and clean.

"Oh, we don't have that in stock anymore," explained Ann O'Nymous , the storeroom supervisor, "we're trying to reduce inventory, and we noticed that this isn't used very often, so we dropped it from our stock. I can order it for you."

"OK, order it then, when will it be in?" asked Aggie nonchalantly.

"Oh, in three, maybe four weeks." Responded Ann.

"Three weeks!? But I need this for my machines NOW," Aggie exploded, "Why does this take so long? Most of this I can get at the local hardware store."

"Oh, I think our stock comes from Bulgaria. We get it pretty cheap you know," Ann said defensively.

"Cheap hell. It won't be cheap when my machine breaks down for lack of its routine PM. Who the hell makes these decisions without talking to the folks who actually do the work?" Aggie said getting increasingly agitated.

"I'll thank you not to swear at me. I don't make these decisions, so don't shoot the messenger. I'm just a peon here doing what I'm told," responded Ann increasingly defensive.

"Crap, go ahead and order what I need. Meantime, I'll get the stuff I need at the hardware, and turn in an expense report for this. Wonder how much that's going to cost to process, not to mention my time not doing what I could be doing" huffed Aggie as he left.

Over in operations the Production Manager, Guda Nuff, was having an intense discussion with the operating supervisors "What's going on with our yields?" he asked sharply, "over the past week they've gone from 95% to near 90%. This is awful. It impacts our scrap, our unit cost per ton, and even our disposal costs."

"Oh, this started when we started using those new raw materials from another supplier. Apparently they're quite a bit cheaper, at least that's what the purchasing guy told me," responded one of the operators.

"Cheaper?" the Guda looked quizzically.

"Oh yeah, we save $50 per ton in raw material costs, so the purchasing guy told me," the supervisor said, with just a touch of sarcasm in his voice.

"Yeah, but our processing costs have gone up about $100 per ton" the Production Manager lamented as he charged off to find someone in purchasing for a chat.

Over in maintenance, a similar discussion was happening.

The Maintenance Manager, Seena Nuff, was asking one of his supervisors "What's going on with all this downtime on the drills? We've spent the past year getting them reconfigured and working really well. Now, all of a sudden we're seeing the unplanned downtime jump from 2% to 10%? What's going on?"

"Oh, that's mostly those new drill bits we're using, not the drills themselves. They're working pretty good, save all the broken bits and dull bits needing to be replaced. Our replacement rate has just about doubled in the past couple weeks," offered the supervisor.

"What? Who made that decision?" Seena went on, clearly perturbed. Incidentally, he'd just had his butt chewed by Guda over all the increased downtime and lost production.

"Well, I reckon purchasing put out this spec that was the same as the old spec and found the drill bits a lot cheaper with their new global supplier, so I'm told anyway," responded the supervisor, "but it sure don't look cheaper to me. We've had to bring in guys on overtime at night to try and solve the complaints from the operators, not to mention the downtime. And, you know what else? Every bit we replace, they report as saving money. The more we break and replace, the more money they 'save'. Ain't that silly?"

Seena left in a huff, saying something about going to find someone in purchasing.

Some weeks later there was a conference where representatives from all the operating plants were assembled, mostly plant and production managers, but a few maintenance and engineering managers as well.

Penny Pincher, the VP of Purchasing, gave a grand speech about the use of supply chain principles and how much money was being saved with the new initiative, showing some $300M in lower costs. She had lunch with the Gunnar Runemhard, VP of Operations, who had the company financials with him, turned to the page that outlines Sales, Costs, and Profits.

Gunnar ponderously looked at Penny and said "Listen Penny, you're saying you've saved the company $300M, but looking at our financials, it's looks to me like our operating costs, and profits, over the past three years are essentially flat, that is, they haven't gone down at all. The $300M has gone missing!! Where'd it go?"

Pincher, obviously flustered, embarrassed, and defensive responded curtly, "I just showed you the numbers. You saw them! I can't help it if the plants spend more money than they should. You should get your operation squared away before jumping me."

After that, the silence was really long and a chill settled into the air. Penny Pincher suddenly had an important meeting to attend, and Gunnar let out a long sigh.

We probably know where the $300M went, don't we?

The Lesson: 1) Everyone must think at a systems level, so that we understand the impact of our decisions on the business system as a whole. 2) Rewards must foster system level performance, not just individual performance.

Managing Spare Parts

4

We've all heard the story that 'For the want of a nail a shoe was lost. For the want of a shoe a horse was lost. For the want of a horse a man was lost. For the want of a man a battle was lost. For the want of a battle a war was lost. And, for the want of a war a country was lost.' Below is the modern day version of that story that reflects the chaos theory behind it.

Webechep was a pretty good company, and was managed by finance and accounting people. They worked really hard to manage cash, to keep expenses down, and generally were quite frugal in their approach. Managing cash and cash flow was particularly high on their proverbial "radar screen".

One area of particular concern was the storeroom at each operation, where all the equipment spares and consumable operating materials were kept. In the mind of the CFO, Ima Moneymaker, this was working capital that clearly was not working. It was just sitting. "Why do we need all that money tied up in parts and materials, when the company needed cash for its ongoing operation?" he mused.

So, he launched a project for reducing working capital. He had each operation report on the issues listed below. Of course he checked the reports with his own analysis, since he really didn't trust the people at the plants. "All they did was SPEND money, he thought, we've got to MAKE money."

1. Inventory turns on spares and stores materials – the amount we spend on parts each year, divided by the average value of how much is kept in the storeroom. The result – stores inventory turns was 0.7. That is,

Webechep kept well over one year's worth of spares in inventory, at least in terms of the financial ratio.

2. Stock that had not been used at all in one year and three years. The result – nearly 55% of the inventory had not been used in three years or more. Nearly 30% had not been used in one year.

3. Some 10% of the stocked items accounted for 90% of the annual expenditure.

4. The material on hand in excess of the maximum quantities stated in the mix/max specification was over 20%.

5. There were several "squirrel stores" or areas in the plant where maintenance kept "stuff" they might need, but that was not being managed by the store room supervisor.

Moneymaker looked at other issues, but these were tops in his mind, and he was discouraged, and later, angry. "Our inventory turns on our products are from 5-15, depending on the product line, and overall it's about 10," he fumed, "we only keep about one month's supply in inventory for production. How come the maintenance guys can't manage as well as production? We need to fix this!"

He went on, growing more animated as he marinated in his own misery, "Why do we need spares that we don't use? We need to get rid of those items which haven't been used in more than 2 years. If they don't use it, they obviously don't need it," he said authoritatively to the nodding heads in his staff meeting.

"And, we need to get our min/max in control. Keeping more than we need is absurd, and this just proves that's what we're doing. And, we need to get these so-called Squirrel Stores under our control."

From there they were off on an improvement effort to reduce their spare parts inventory. Moneymaker reckoned he could reduce that by at least $5M over the next year. Incidentally, reducing inventory was one of his key performance indicators for his annual bonus. Having done the numbers in his head, he also reckoned achieving that target would be worth $20,000 on his performance bonus.

So, they went to work, cutting back on maximum quantities, demanding that the staff eliminate those items they weren't using at least every two years, demanding that the operations use the vendors on the corporate approved vendor list, and only ordering the parts needed when needed from those vendors. In some cases this was acceptable – the vendor was in the same area and could respond relatively quickly, *except* on weekends, and at nights, and on holidays, and whenever certain people didn't show up for work, and when... Anyway, in other cases, it was more difficult, since the closest offices for the corporate approved vendors were in another city, or in some cases another state, or in one or two cases in another country.

"How far can Mexico be from the US?" he wondered about the operation across the border from San Diego, "Crap, you can see the plant from San Diego. They'll work it out." He didn't *think* customs would be much of a problem, but he never did check.

Meanwhile, as Moneymaker continued with his working capital improvement (inventory reduction) program, the operations had an entirely different perspective.

"What's going on?" asked the maintenance manager, Pistan Brok, to no one in particular, as he walked by the storeroom.

"Oh," responded Fitwell, a mechanic, "they're taking stuff out of inventory that hasn't been used in over two years. Got some sorta deal with the vendors to take it back, but I heard that some of it is going to the scrap heap. Doesn't make sense, givin' back or throwin' away all that stuff we've already paid for. I guess that's the high finance that I don't understand."

Concerned, Pistan went into the store room and asked for the supervisor. Incidentally, the store room supervisor reported to the purchasing manager, who reported to the CFO.

"What's going on here?" he asked.

Spiffy, the store room supervisor responded, somewhat perplexed, "Well, the boss (referring to Moneymaker) said we had to unload anything that hadn't been used in over two years and sent us a list of all that. Some of it is going back to the vendor, and some of it is going to the scrap yard. Some of it, I don't know exactly where it's going. Anyway, those were his orders."

"No one asked me about any of this. How did he know what to eliminate?" retorted Pistan.

Spiffy, now a bit on the defensive - "Oh, he and the accounting guys here sorted through all the parts in the catalog and said these were the ones. Didn't you get that email that went out?"

Pistan was now really concerned, offering a weak reply.

"I've been on vacation the past two weeks. My email is overloaded with messages, most of which I've ignored. Apparently this is one of them. Could you give me a list of the stuff that's being removed?"

"Of course," said Spiffy, "but most of it is already gone. Moneymaker put an "urgent" on this. Said he had some sort of board meeting at the end of the month and wanted a full tally of what we'd managed to do."

"Oh crap," thought Pistan.

He took the list and went back to his guys. Several of the parts that had been returned or scrapped were for critical machinery that was still in the plant.

Fitwell chirped up, "I'm no genius, but if it hadn't broken in over two years, that's good news isn't it – we haven't needed to fix it. But, if it does break, we better have the parts we need to get it back on line. Otherwise, we won't be producing much, but we'll still be paying people to stand around. Who makes these decisions anyway?"

All Pistan could do was shrug. He went on to observe, "Apparently Moneymaker does, without consulting any of us so-called users. He apparently doesn't understand the concept of managing risk either – the risk of lost production and reduced efficiency."

Fitwell sputtered sarcastically "I just wonder how much all this will save us. Every time some dumbass does something like this, we have to pay for it. I'll bet within a week we'll need one of those parts they just dumped. Damn it!"

As we all know, Murphy (of Murphy's Laws) was an optimist, and within the month one of the critical machines crashed unexpectedly. And... yep, it needed one of the parts that hadn't been used in years, and had been eliminated from the storeroom.

The good news though is that the vendor still had the part, and found it after much searching, and sold it back to Webechep, but for about 10 times what they paid in scrap value. And they only lost 36 hours of production, worth about $5,000 per hour, or about $180,000.

After this, Fitwell decided to take matters into his own hands. He had been around for decades, and had seen this type thing before. "Just another manager in a long line of managers trying to make points with somebody," he thought to himself.

Anyway, he knew how to buy things on a direct purchase order, or with the company credit card, using standard vendor systems. He knew how to work the system to get what he wanted. So he met privately with Pistan and after reviewing the list of things that had been removed, they decided that certain of these items were critical to managing the risk of failure in the operation. They might not need them, but if they did, they couldn't wait for a week to get them from some vendor in another state.

Besides several of those vendors had promised to stock items, but when it came to needing them, they were out about 20% of the time. Fitwell had kept a log of their performance. So, over about six months, they ordered the things they thought were needed, just under the radar so to speak, and returned essentially all the material they thought had been mistakenly eliminated from the store room. But, rather than have old Moneymaker get into their stuff again, they created a "*secret squirrel store*", a place where they kept stuff, just in case.

All was well and good until Fitwell went on vacation, and Pistan left the company. Squirrel stores weren't really managed, and memories have a pretty short half-life.

All in all the company suffered. Parts were eliminated to reduce working capital, but many of those parts had helped minimize the risk of lost production, and maintenance inefficiency. Some of those same parts were needed shortly after, and cost the company nearly $200,000 to replenish. The other parts worked their way back into the operation (the "squirrel store" returned but was even more secretive), but weren't set up in a system to be effectively managed; and more space was used; and more expense was incurred.

Moneymaker got his bonus based on excellent performance. It wasn't much of a moneymaker though, was it?

The Lesson: The risk of production and efficiency losses must be balanced against capital costs. Capital is easy to measure. Risk isn't. Both have to be managed. 2) The people doing the work will follow their natural inclination to manage risk with excess capital; or manage capital with excess risk. 3) For each equipment, ask "What fails most often, and when it does, what parts do we need?" Make sure you have those.

Install and Startup
With Discipline

5

Waggawagga was having difficulty in one of its key operations. They were in the middle of a shutdown for their flagship plant to install and startup a major capital project, one which represented new technology and production capability. This new technology was supposed to give them a critical advantage in cost and quality.

Coincidentally, while the plant was down, they had decided to do several major maintenance projects in older areas of the plant, things that had been delayed for some time and now seemed the opportune time for this. But, things were not going well in either area. As you might expect, there was a lot of pressure to "get the plant back on line" and they had already missed two deadlines for this. Each time they thought they were ready, some little something, e.g., a valve improperly set to purge a line, or a set point on an instrument being incorrect and tripping the system. Each event seemed trivial, but each created a delay in startup, as they resolved the problem. They were now over a month behind on the original schedule for returning the older part of the plant; and over two months behind the project schedule for starting the new part of the plant; customers were beginning to get upset about promised deliveries; inventories were getting dangerously low; and cost overruns were mounting.

Gus Giterdon, the commissioning manager, was known for his ability to get things done. He was very results oriented and had an excellent grasp of all the technologies, and, had good project systems in place for managing them, i.e., Pert/Gantt charts and critical path mapping, work breakdown structure, good procurement interface, and so on.

He had managed similar projects. He also had a relatively good working relationship with the contractor. They had worked on other contracts together and had been reasonably successful. At least that was the perception.

Quonso Qwikfix, the maintenance manager handling all the maintenance work in parallel, also had a relatively good reputation for getting work done. He was highly responsive to production, and had been at the plant for nearly 10 years.

Before the shutdown, there had been a lot of pressure to shut down on the date scheduled. Giterdon had been adamant that the project was to be done on schedule. Unfortunately, the plant had a critical customer delivery they had to make before shutting down, and because of other problems in making those (raw material supply and equipment failures) Kep Inkuntrol, the production manager had contacted Giterdon about delaying the shutdown for two days to get the orders out for the customer, and properly bring down the plant.

Giterdon had not been happy about this, "You've got to hand the plant over on time," he demanded.

"But," Kep responded, a bit of desperation in his voice, "I've got these orders to fill first, and then I have to take some of this equipment down very slowly. Otherwise, we can induce a lot of problems on startup."

"That's your problem," Giterdon replied, sensing his schedule was about to be impacted, "you committed to the date, now meet the date!"

Kep contacted his boss, and soon found himself on a three-way call with the VP of manufacturing, Ob Sessive, who simply said "I expect you to hand the plant over on the date agreed."

With that Kep went about completing the order and shutting the plant down, quickly, but knowing some of the machinery needed a slow cool down, and some of the process lines would likely foul up because of this. He had protested to the VP, who was new to the business and didn't seem to fully appreciate his protests. "Maybe I didn't get my point across very well," Kep thought to himself as he was getting everybody working on shutting down, but only over several protests.

Meanwhile, Quonso, wasn't having much luck either. There seemed to be a lot of failures after the work was, he thought, done. They had found a leak in one of the vessels when they tried to startup, something that hadn't even been worked on. It turned out the quick shutdown had caused a thermally induced crack in the vessel near a joint. That repair took a long time since it was an uncommon alloy, and it wasn't in his budget either. Other problems crept up – excess fouling in some of the lines was a problem, along with some of the instrument lines plugging, requiring extra cleaning, and more time. There was a long list of seemingly simple issues like this, all of which were delaying his part of the startup effort. Cost overruns were getting way out of line too.

Quonso had also tried to coordinate his efforts with Giterdon, who was lukewarm to the coordination effort. Giterdon thought all that coordination would only slow down his project, and he certainly didn't want that. "Couldn't Quonso just do his part without bothering people on his project?" He asked, but only to himself.

Quonso also had a less than sterling opinion of Giterdon and his contractor. He thought the contractor's whole objective was to "get in, get out, and get paid".

He'd had to come in after other projects and spent a small fortune correcting errors and making things right, all after the contractor had been paid and was gone. He had some resentment toward Giterdon, and vice versa, so the working relationship was lukewarm at best.

In any event, in the new project there were several piping, instrument, and wiring connections into the existing equipment, and Quonso was working on three of these systems during the shutdown where this would occur. It would be wrong to say they had no coordination, but the extent of it was pretty superficial, e.g., we'll be working on this on that day and will have this and that off for testing, and we should be done on this day. There was no detailed review of drawings, diagrams, procedures, and so on to make sure that the work on the three systems that both groups were working on was developed and coordinated in great detail. By the way, some of the maintenance work was actually minor capital work – updating and minor modifications of old equipment.

Well, Murphy's laws were active on these minor modifications. Giterdon called Quonso one day and the following conversation ensued.

Giterdon demanded "What happened to that piping, P12 and P14, and wiring, EL256 and 321, we were connecting into over on Unit 3? The drawings said one thing, but when the contractor went to do the work, the equipment had changed. What's going on?"

"Oh, we had to bring the piping and wiring up to code. That's been in the works for about a year now," Quonso said, confused at Giterdon's hostility.

"Why didn't you tell me you were doing that?" Giterdon's voice was getting a tiny bit louder.

"We did," responded Qwikfix.

"Did not," Giterdon responded childishly.

"Did too," Quonso took the bait, sustaining the childishness.

Giterdon blurted, "You told me you were going to change it out. You didn't say you were going to change the piping material to hasteloy. That's pretty exotic stuff for our contractor. And you sure as hell didn't say you were going to change the entire wiring configuration and all the junction boxes. You even added another instrument control line."

"That line is part of a new protection system for shutting the equipment down if we have an excursion. I tried to get you to let me sit with your engineers and outline all this, but NOooo," he mocked, "You didn't want to spend the money or have us slow down your project. You said you could handle it," retorted Quonso. The conversation deteriorated from there.

None of this improved their relationship. Several weeks, and much gnashing of the teeth later the plant was finally back on line, with huge overruns on both capital and maintenance costs, and relationships severely bruised.

The Lessons: Old ones - 1) The devil is indeed in the details. 2) Coordination among task interdependent groups is essential. 3) If you have procedures, follow them, or you'll pay later.

Operate With Care

6

Ilkoara Corporation was a good company. They had been in business for decades, and were typically at least average, and often better than average in their financial performance measures. As with most businesses, they had weathered a few storms and come out of it in reasonably good condition.

However, the recent market downturn was much more severe than any of the historical ones, and on top of that competitors from China were making inroads into some of their base customers with comparable products. The senior executives did not view these Chinese products as "comparable", and often made snide remarks about their quality.

Yet, their top three customers, who were retailers that represented some 60% of their business in one product line, thought they should give the Chinese products a try. These retailers then positioned the products for sale to their customers. After all, if *their customers* considered the Chinese products comparable, would it really matter what Ilkoara's senior management thought? And if so, Ilkoara would be under even more pressure on pricing, quality, and delivery. Capitalism is such a cruel economic model.

Of course as all companies do, Ilkoara was working to reduce its costs, improve its quality and delivery, and was also reviewing all its products to determine if there were any opportunities for rationalization. Over the years, it seemed that many products had been added, but few had been dropped, and so this deserved some scrutiny, especially since the manufacturing managers had complained loudly about the cost of some products that were being ordered.

And, as you might expect, Mark Eting, the VP of marketing complained about the performance of the manufacturing people. A meeting of the minds seemed appropriate.

While all this was going on, the VP of Manufacturing, Otto Kratic, thought it was time for a major strategic review of their manufacturing practices. While he disagreed with some of the accusations being leveled at manufacturing, he thought they should have their house in order as they engaged the marketing folks in a debate about product mix, customers, costs, quality, and delivery.

Meanwhile, at the manufacturing plants, and in particular at the Horshoky plant, the most practical way to describe the culture on the shop floor, and in particular the relationship between production and maintenance, was one of "We break'em; you fix'em".

Beau Bricksworth, a mechanic on one of the lines, was quite frustrated with this attitude. Beau (often called Brick as a nickname, and if you could see him, you'd understand why) hated being called in at night to "fix things". Though he was quite good at his work, being a master craftsman and having the respect of all his peers, he thought all the call-ins were a waste of money, and more importantly, his time.

He often lamented "Why can't we just stop breaking them?" And, even though the extra money was a benefit, he just didn't like waking up in the middle of the night to go fix something. Besides he opined "That's when I'm the tiredest, and might make more mistakes." He actually longed for a boring month.

Beau had also recently been to a seminar that showed compelling data that more than two-thirds (67%) of equipment failures were due to poor operating practice such as poor changeovers and setups, improper startup and shutdown, running the machinery outside its operating envelope, not keeping the machine clean, or tightening down loose fasteners, or not giving the machine a squirt of oil or grease every now and again. He could relate to all the examples the presenter offered. On top of that he observed that there were eight times more operators than maintenance technicians.

Beau was not a mathematical genius, but he thought "I can't fix'em faster than they can break'em. There are eight times more of them (referring to operators) than there are of us. If we could just get them to do start up, shut down, and operate the equipment with care, and maybe some simple maintenance and basic care only just a tiny bit of time, that would more than double the number of people looking after the machinery, and stop a lot of failures. I always thought maintenance was about keeping things running, not fixing things."

Unfortunately his view was among those of a very small minority.

Around this time, the plant manager, Bob Inweave, came in to the plant early one morning, and was asking about shipments of a product to a key customer. Apparently he had a call the night before, at home, from that customer regarding a critical shipment. They hadn't received it and he wanted to know the status. These were critical raw material parts to their manufacturing process, and if they didn't get them in the next 24 hours, the customer's entire operation would have to shut down.

Incidentally, Bob had been away to a corporate meeting the past couple days to review the plant's performance. He was under a lot of pressure to improve the plant. With the travel schedule and the all-day meetings, he'd been out of touch with the plant and had told them that he only wanted to be contacted in the event of a true emergency. And, while he was gone, one of the sales force had called, demanding that one of his customers get priority on a shipment.

In retrospect, it appears that he was trying to impress the customer with the quick response he could get from the company. While that's not a bad thing, unfortunately, his shipment displaced the other critical shipment for the customer that Bob was asking about. Apparently one of the shipping clerks had been sick and hadn't tagged that order as critical. And, on top of it all, yes, you guessed it, the plant went down for eight hours, and even further delayed production and shipment.

Now, as they say, all hell was breaking loose. Bob was also getting calls from Otto about this order. The customer had called Otto as well, at home. And, to top it off, this wasn't the first time something like this had happened. Over the past year, they had several similar incidents, and that was the reason Bob was out of the plant in the first place, to advise his boss of his plans to get things corrected. This incident just didn't help at all, not his plant, not his customers, nor his career. Whew!!

Bob called a meeting with Dan Driver, his production manager, and Mike Mekanik, his maintenance manager, to discuss the problems they are having, the pressure he is under and how they might correct the situation. The meeting did not go well.

Dan, who indeed is a driven individual, launched into a defensive diatribe, "Damn it Bob, you're always on my case to get stuff out the door. And your threats if I don't are not all that subtle. And, you're constantly moving the mark. One day this is the priority, the next day another thing is the priority", he seethed.

"Make up your mind and stick to it. It wouldn't surprise me at all if we have this meeting again tomorrow, but with a different, and new priority. All I'm doing is following *your orders.*" Dan put a lot of emphasis on YOUR ORDERS, implying the problems were Bob's fault. The room grew really quiet now.

Bob's face turned really red as he went to slow-burn mode, but he held back for the time being. "Let him get it off his chest", he thought.

Mike jumped in about now to break the ice, though he wasn't quite sure where this meeting was going. "Can we talk about how we're going to address our problems?" he asked.

"These **are** our problems," retorted Dan, who seemed to be on a roll for getting things off his chest. "And by the way, if you'd just fix things right, our problems wouldn't be nearly as bad as they are".

Bob was thinking, "Maybe we should take a timeout."

As he was about to open his mouth, Mike made a "T" sign with his hands. "Can we all just take a deep breath here?" he asked.

And everyone did.

Mike reflected on what Beau showed him and said "Look, I've seen some data that says two-thirds of production losses have nothing to do with the equipment. It's mostly things like product changeovers, raw material quality and quantity and rate and quality losses."

"Bull crap," Dan interjected defensively.

"Let him finish," Bob said sternly. Clearly Bob was getting frustrated with Dan's attitude.

Mike continued, "…and, of the production losses that **are** equipment related, two-thirds of the equipment failures are due to poor operating practice such as improper startup and shutdown, running the machinery outside its operating envelope, not keeping the machine clean, or tightening down loose fasteners, or not giving the machine a squirt of oil or grease every now and again."

"Greasing is **your** job," Dan interjected once again, though not quite as strongly.

"Granted," Mike continued, "And we'll keep doing that, but think about this, we have eight times more operators than maintenance technicians. If this data applies to us, we can't possibly keep up with the defects being introduced by poor operation."

"BULL CRAP," exploded Dan, "Where do you get this data?"

Mike squeezed in "According to Beau…" before being interrupted by Dan, again.

"Beau! Who the hell is Beau? What does he know? Beau is just a mechanic."

Mike continued more forcefully "Yes, but he's a damn good one, and he's pulled your ass out of the fire any number of times, so we should give him the benefit of the doubt on this."

Seeing things start to escalate yet again, Bob jumped in signally a big "T" for time out, "All right, I've heard enough. Both of you look at me, and don't interrupt. I want you to go get data on our production losses. We're supposed to be tracking asset utilization and overall equipment effectiveness, so I want to see data, and I want this arguing to stop, NOW. You two go *work together* to get me the data related to Mike's points. I'm emphasizing the words ***work together*** if you hadn't noticed, because if you don't, one or both of you aren't going to be here much longer," though he was looking directly at Dan when he uttered the last phrase.

He continued, "Not only that, but to help you work together, I'm going to hold you **both** accountable for unplanned downtime, maintenance costs, and on-time delivery. And, from this time forward, I can, and will, reverse your roles, at a moment's notice. Think about the consequences of that!"

"But, I don't control delivery times," objected Mike.

"Yeah, but if you insist on doing PM and it affects delivery, I want you to have to think twice, and work with Dan," replied Bob calmly.

"But, I don't control maintenance costs," objected Dan.

"Yeah, but if your people aren't operating the equipment properly, and that causes failures and costs, I want you to think twice," Bob replied calmly once again.

"Now both of you go cool off. I'll see you both back here on Friday, with data, and a plan for working together! At that meeting you just may get to take on each other's role. "

Bob was right – they had the data on production losses and asset utilization. But, nobody was paying any particular attention to it. It was reported to headquarters, where a bunch of corporate staff looked at it and harped about how badly they were doing. They were like seagulls – swoop, poop, and squawk. What did they know? It was easy to throw rocks, when you didn't have to do anything about the problems. And besides, who had time, considering all the problems they had, to analyze the data?

On Friday, they met again. Dan had calmed down, and Mike seemed calm as well. They walked in together, having just met before the meeting with Bob to review what they were going to say. Apparently, the message to work together had been received by both of them.

Dan started, "Well, I'm embarrassed to say it, but Mike is right, or at least right enough to have made his point. About 60% of our production losses aren't related to the equipment breaking down. It's things like changeovers, and one he didn't mention that's at the root cause is production planning. In particular, it looks like the sales department calls in almost daily to interrupt our production plans for the week, resulting in more changeovers. Frankly, we're not very good at these. I've complained about this for a long time, but I didn't realize the total impact it was having, an hour at a time. We've tried to be cooperative with sales, sometimes to a fault. It's that 'customer driven' thing we try to live by. But, it's killing us from a production standpoint."

He paused, then, "Mike and I don't agree on the breakdown of the other 40% of the equipment breakdowns, no pun intended, but even if the equipment breakdowns are because half my guys are not operating properly, and half his guys not fixing properly, maintenance still only controls 20% of our production losses."

"Hmmm," nodded Bob.

"Remember Dan, you've got eight times as many operators as I have techs, and they break equipment all the time." interjected Mike, somewhat abruptly, and perhaps taking the offensive for a change.

Bob intervened, "Dan's making your point for you Mike. Don't interrupt him."

"Sorry," Mike apologized, looking at the floor.

"So, now that we know this, what are we going to do?" quizzed Bob. There was a long pause, with Bob waiting to see what his key staff thought.

Finally, Mike spoke up hesitantly, "Well let's start by working *together* to try to resolve some of these problems," stressing the word together, "For too long, we've tended to blame one another, sometimes in kidding around, sometimes in more heated accusations. That doesn't seem to have worked. I'll get with my guys and ask them, first off, about their problems, about what we're doing wrong, and what operations is doing wrong."

At this point, Dan interjected defensively, "I thought you just said we're going to work together and not play the blame game."

Mike responded calmly this time, "I'm just going to look for information I can share with you, so we can solve problems together. We've done our fair share of screw-ups, and I'll lay those on the table, but I need your help to resolve some of the problems we see with how the equipment is being operated. I'm looking for information to help us work together."

Dan seemed to calm down, responding, "OK, I'll do the same.

"Good!" Bob finally said, "Let's meet again next week, and review where we are on this, and begin to develop our plan of action. In the meantime, I'm going to have a look at the data Dan just presented on production planning and sales intervening into our production schedule to see if we can do something about that. I'll share what I've learned next week."

In subsequent weeks and months, everyone used the data and information to prioritize actions and resolve problems. Yes, they had the occasional dustup and reverted to their old forms, but Bob, with Mike's help, soon changed the whole atmosphere from 'we break'em, you fix'em' to 'let's work together to solve problems'. And, perhaps more importantly, and with considerable difficulty, Dan began to assume the leadership role for the stability and reliability of the plant, and stopped blaming Mike for every equipment failure.

Bob continued to field questions and demands from his boss, Otto Kratic. These were sometimes intense, but he held his ground, providing data, action plans and measures of improvement that were trending upward, and building Otto's confidence in their efforts. Perhaps as importantly, he got Mark's help in addressing the issue of product mix, eliminating many of the "dogs" in their offering, and sales routinely attempting to change the production schedule. These attempted interventions became the exception, not the rule.

In time, on time delivery went from 89% to 95%, OEE went from 61% to 72%, scrap and rework were cut in half, and more importantly, unit costs dropped by nearly 10%, creating substantially better gross profits. While these were still not world class numbers, they were so much better than before. Indeed the plant received an award for "most improved".

Unfortunately, all this good performance led to Dan being "pinched" by another company and leaving, and Bob getting a promotion to a senior staff role reporting to Otto, supporting all plants in the improvement process. Mike, ever steady, remained with the plant. A new plant manager and production manager soon arrived, and the cycle began yet again. "Just more people to train," thought Mike. But then, that's another story.

The Lessons: 1) It's ok to focus on your job and do it well, but when doing that affects other departments, it's time to pause and think about the overall impact on the business of your actions and behavior. Work together, using data, to get better results. 2) "Take care of the place where you make your living, so it will take care of you."

Maintenance –
Maintaining or Fixing?

7

"Accordin' to this Webster's dictionary, maintain means to preserve from failure or decline," Phil Osifer, one of the senior mechanics at Girringun Company, thought out loud to no one in particular. Phil tended to wax eloquent at times (or was it wax elephants?).

"Here he goes again," Skip Tikell whispered, also thinking out loud, as he was trying to gather his tools and PPE (personal protective equipment), for a job they'd just been assigned. Skip liked Phil, but sometimes the pontificating was annoying.

"What difference does it make?" Skip asked Phil abruptly.

"I don't think our management understands the definition of maintenance. If they did, we'd spend less time fixin' things and more time preservin'em," Phil observed dryly.

"Yeah, so when's that gonna happen? When you tell'em?" countered Skip, ever the skeptic.

"Hard to say, but in the meantime, we'll just keep fixin'em. Don't really have much choice do we?" Phil looked into Skip's eyes, almost as a challenge. "Well, do we?" he asked.

"I guess not," Skip responded, but then quickly thought, "Oh crap, here we go again, another philosophical debate, and I took the bait by answering."

"We **do** have a choice don't we, to tell'em or not to tell'em?" Phil paraphrased Shakespeare, as he was wont to do.

"Yeah, we've got a choice, like it matters. We've chased this rabbit before, and it keeps gettin' away. So, what would we tell'em **this** time?" Skip responded with his most frustrated voice, having been down this road several times before.

"Well, you know, we just put in this computerized maintenance management system this year to help us manage our work, and plan and schedule the work better. But it's gotten worse! Now, we've got four guys planning work that we don't do. We'd be better off if they were available to help with the work, instead of planning work that we don't seem to ever get to. This happens every single week – we've got all these plans, but we never get to more than half of the work that's planned. Every day the plan gets interrupted to go do something that's not in the plan, **every day!** What good is a plan if we don't follow it. Wouldn't it be better if we eliminated the un-plannable work? We aren't going to get any better if the defects and problems that come in every day keep overwhelming our plans." Phil was on a roll now, and all Skip could do was listen.

Phil continued, "Drucker said there's nothing worse than doing more efficiently work that you shouldn't have to do in the first place. Why don't we stop the defects that are causing the work in the first place? Why don't we focus on preventing the failures instead of fixing the failures more efficiently? Why don't we get operators to run the machines right and take care of them, so we don't have as many failures? Why don't we get the design right so we don't have as many failures? Why don't we have the right parts when we need them, so we don't have to use substitutes that break more often? When we do have to fix things, how come we never have enough time to fix'em right, but we always have enough time to fix'em again?" Phil paused to take a breath. Even he could see that he was up on his soapbox, and probably should lighten up.

But he couldn't help himself, "And management is always bitching about how much money we spend in maintenance. We're not maintainin', we're fixin'. There ought to be a Fixin' Budget and a Maintainin' Budget. We don't control most of the Fixin' Budget. Seventy percent of the time the fixin' is needed because somebody upstream screwed up and broke it. Then we have to fix it, and to add insult to injury, we get **charged** for the fixin', not them. It's just wrong."

"You done?" asked Skip politely.

"For now, thanks for listening… let's go to work and do what we *can* do, and not worry too much about what we *can't* do." Phil smiled as he said it. Skip knew it wouldn't be the last time. Phil just needed to vent sometimes.

The business continued with its mediocrity, but most other companies were the same way, so at least they had competitive parity.

The Lessons: 1) To maintain is to preserve from failure or decline, **not** to fix. 2) If the defects occurring outside maintenance overwhelm maintenance plans, planning will never be effective. 3) Don't let what you can't do be an excuse for not doing what you can do.

Epilogue: Drucker did in fact say "There is nothing so useless as doing efficiently that which should not be done at all." So, it's essential that we eliminate the defects upstream, in design, procurement and operations, that cause the work to be necessary in maintenance as part of improving the maintenance process.

Sustenance Capital and Investment Capital – Both Are Investments

8

"What's that smell?" asked Olf Ackteri, as he scrunched his nose and looked quizzically at Al Armid.

"Oh, one of the storage tanks must've sprung another leak. It's not dangerous. It just smells funny. It happens every few months, and we go in and patch it, and hope for another few months before the next one," Al cynically responded, "Those damn things really need to be replaced, but management keeps delaying it. I reckon they think we can patch'em forever."

"What do the neighbors say?" Olf asked, since the plant was literally just a few hundred yards from a residential area.

"Oh, they complain to the locals, and there's a big hearing with the town council, and we promise not to do it again… and then do it again," Al observed. Going on, with a sense of resignation, "You'd think somebody on the council is on our payroll. Not only that, have you seen the roof in our warehouse where we keep all our inventory. It's full of holes. I guess none of the leaks are over our products."

Meanwhile the engineering manager, Erasmus B. Hurtin, is working really hard to get his new capital plan improved. He had repeatedly included capital to replace the tanks, and to replace the warehouse roof, where frequent leaks could damage finished products. He was also worried about their license to operate, and long term health effects on employees.

The tanks didn't contain anything explosive, or particularly toxic, but Erasmus was concerned that repeated exposure to these hydrocarbons might affect people's well-being, not just be a nuisance. And, at times they had affected production, since the tanks weren't available for storage during the patching process.

Each time he had raised these concerns, his voice had been silenced with a curt "These products are used as food ingredients, for goodness sake, they're not harmful."

It was interesting to Erasmus that he hadn't had much trouble getting capital for new process equipment that helped improve production. The return on investment, even if a bit uncertain, was easy enough to demonstrate.

But, these damn tanks, and the roof, were another matter. He had repeatedly been denied capital for these, and told to "Just fix'em. We don't have the money for new tanks," or words to that effect. He was becoming increasingly frustrated with the position being taken by each new executive.

Recently, the company had been sold, yet again, to Renuzem Company. Erasmus thought, "Here we go again, another owner, wonder if what the odds are for them approving capital for the new tanks?"

Steeling himself for the pending rejection, he had recently had a conversation with the new CEO, Ben Longfellow, the newest among a series of CEO's, since the company had been bought and sold four times over the past 8 years. Fortunately for Erasmus, he had survived each purchase, unlike many of his associates. He wasn't sure if he lived a charmed life, or not.

Erasmus pleaded his case, "Look Mr. Longfellow, for years now we've been pleading for the money to fix the leaks in these tanks, and to get the roof fixed. Every time, the new owners have rejected our requests, but the risks are increasing, with every day. Look at this!" he exclaimed, placing several pictures of the tanks and roof before Longfellow. Large holes were apparent in each picture.

"Well, haven't you patched these?" demanded Longfellow.

Erasmus sighed, "Of course we have, but every time we patch, a new leak pops up within months, sometimes even weeks. These tanks are just one crappy design to start with. They should have been stainless, or at least coated steel, because the vapors of the liquid are slightly acidic, and that corrodes the tanks, but whoever put the tanks in didn't want to spend the extra money. And, they've been here 15 years."

He paused to let that sink in, "So, we started having these leaks about 5 years ago, and we've been patching ever since. We've done enough patching to pay for new tanks, and our biggest cost is the production we lose as we jigger our storage requirements while we're patching. And, look at the latest ultrasound thickness measurements on the tank dome and sidewalls. They are just horrible. Look…" he said as he showed Longfellow the report and graphs.

Longfellow barely understood what he was looking at. "Put this into plain words for me," he said sternly.

"The tanks walls and dome are becoming so thin, we're at risk of them collapsing," Erasmus responded, all the while thinking to himself "Is that plain enough for you?"

"Why didn't you tell someone this?" demanded Longfellow.

Erasmus was exasperated at the question, giving Longfellow a stern look. He responded curtly, "I've been telling senior management this for years, but every time it comes up, their first question is 'can you patch it?', or 'how much longer will it last?' We've been bought and sold so many times, and each new owner is just unwilling to put any money into things like this. There's no ROI on it. And, when they decide to sell, they sure as hell don't want to put any money into things like this. So, we continue to patch." He continued with a similar discussion about the roof.

At the end of it all, Longfellow was pretty frustrated. He was new, and had been given the task of making the operation profitable, but hadn't been advised of a pending multimillion dollar expenditure. Apparently that was missed, or ignored, in the due diligence process. He thought aloud to himself and to Erasmus "This has the potential to shut us down, and even get our operating license revoked."

"Ya think?" Erasmus responded without thinking much about the cynicism in his voice.

"I can't just go to my board with a request for a blank check, asking for millions that aren't in our capital budget. Put together a plan for me and *a business case*", Ben emphasized, "the risk of collapse, the cost of collapse, including potential production losses, the cost and timing of their replacement, and I want all this in the next week," directed Longfellow.

Erasmus did the analysis Ben had requested, reckoning that there was better than a 20% chance one of the tanks could collapse in the next few months, and that probability increased with time. If it happened, they would lose at least one month's production, worth at least $20 million, not to mention the ill will with their customers, and the cost of a new tank that they would have to install then.

With the business case in hand, Ben proceeded to call an emergency meeting of the board, and ultimately received approval for the replacement and the sustenance capital, avoiding a potentially major catastrophe for the business.

The Lesson: Sustenance capital is just as important as investment capital. Both assure the future of the business.

Operational Autonomy without Financial Autonomy – A Formula for Failure

9

Basic Metals, or BM, is a company that makes, as you've likely guessed, basic metals. Their products are used in any number of industries, that is, automotive, aeronautics, and consumer products, just to name a few. Their products are used by other companies to make the things we buy. You've probably used something today that has the metals they sell.

There is a high degree of variability in the performance of their many operations. The performance across their operating plants ranges from very poor (dangerously so in some cases) to excellent, as demonstrated by a number of measures – unit cost, safety, environmental performance, etc. As you might expect, the worst ones are typically nasty and have low morale, while the best ones are very neat, clean and people are highly motivated. Why is this, that within a single organization, you can have such a wide range of performance? Aren't they driven by the same policies, standards, and practices; and leadership? And, if so, shouldn't the results at each of the plants be substantially closer to the mean? Part of the explanation may be in the story below.

BM's Dependence Plant

Cal Ishnikov, the plant manager, liked for things to go well at BM's Dependence Plant, and he drove himself really hard to meet all the company's demands, including all the new initiatives. At one recent manager's meeting, he was quizzed by Willy Nilly, one of the production supervisors.

"Boss, have you read the new corporate directive about using best practice and applying the Toyota Production System, what we're calling Basic's Production Management System, or Basic's PMS?" inquired Willy, one of the production supervisors.

"Yeah, I've read it, some good stuff in there, but right now I'm more worried about how we're going to make production quota's this month," responded Cal.

"So, you think best practice is a good thing?" countered Willy, sensing a bit of reluctance in Cal's voice.

"Yes, I do," Cal responded curtly, then going on, "But, right now I've got five different best practice initiatives being thrown at me, one for safety, one for maintenance, one for environmental, one even for accounting, and now this one, and we don't really have time to give them all the attention they need. We've gotta do what we've gotta do **right now,** and not get too distracted by one more initiative."

"Oh," Willy said sheepishly, backing off his initial enthusiasm. "So, what are we going to do?

"Whatever I damn well say," Cal quickly replied, and then continued, "Everybody here already has a full-time job, so all these initiatives add more work, but not more people. Corporate has one person driving each initiative, and that person thinks they're the most important person in the world. I just wish they'd get off my ass. They're like damn seagulls – they swoop, poop, and squawk. Then, they go back to corporate and tell management how bad we smell. Of course we smell bad – they just crapped all over us, but they didn't help us get the practices in place. They don't give a rat's ass how we get it all done."

Perhaps Cal needed to vent a little. He was obviously frustrated.

"So, are we doing this one? Or not?" Willy asked, almost wishing he hadn't, after he asked.

"I'll let you know," Cal replied, abruptly ending the conversation.

With his keen sense for the obvious, Willy decided not to pursue this topic any further, but he did need to know about a capital improvement, and a new hire he was hoping to get on board. So, he went on, "By the way Boss, did we get approval for the $50K capital project for upgrading these instruments?" pointing to a panel drawing.

"No, damn it." Cal was still pretty frustrated from the first line of questioning. "They have all these initiatives, with all these people on me about each one, but when I ask for one tiny bit of extra capital, it's turned down. That project had a payback of one year, but it still wasn't good enough. You'd think I'd have a little more authority and autonomy for a plant that's worth over $500M. $50K is 0.01% of what this plant's worth."

Willy was thinking about his next question, reluctant to continue, but then deciding to go ahead. They were already into it, so why not get it over with he was thinking. "How about that new outside operator we've been asking for to help with the routines for checking and lubing the equipment?" Willy asked softly, knowing the answer, but wanting to confirm it.

"No, that's been disapproved too," Cal responded with a tone of resignation. "Same logic on that, we've got 600 people here including contractors. You'd think I would have the authority to hire one person I consider critical, and even manage the 600 within 10-20 people, so long as I deliver on the products, quality, and gross profits. Apparently not," he finished. "I've got to get to my next meeting," he said as he waved good bye.

Cal and the Dependence plant floundered along, trying to do all the initiatives, but doing them all relatively poorly. No additional people were added at the corporate level to support the deployment of the initiatives, so the seagull approach continued, frustrating nearly everyone.

Meanwhile, the capital project for the improved instrumentation lingered along in limbo, along with the proposed new technician for helping keep the equipment in better operating condition. The Dependence plant continued with its mediocre performance, never getting really good at anything in particular, since it never had the focus, or autonomy to do this.

BM's Independence Plant

At another division of BM, the senior management, and particularly the President, Willie B. Difernt, was taking a different approach, giving more autonomy to the plant managers. After all, he reasoned, if you couldn't give some latitude and autonomy to the plant manager for hiring and capital, then you likely had the wrong person running the plant.

So, he decided to give the plant manager a range of 3% on hiring, that is, as long as he kept his headcount, including full-time-equivalent contractors, within ± 3% of the agreed numbers, he could hire and fire without prior approval, so long as everything was consistent with other corporate personnel policies. The range on capital was limited to 0.05% of the plant's replacement value, but that was still $250K.

At the same time, the plant manager would be held accountable to deliver on the business results, that is, gross profit, quality, delivery, and safety.

On the other hand, Willie was convinced that a best practice model was essential for their future prosperity, so he was insistent that those be clearly defined, and applied, and not optional. That is, once they were defined, they were required by the plants, and built into their ISO 9002 certification. More importantly, he provided the resources at the corporate level to help each plant apply the standard for each practice. When corporate "initiators" reviewed these best practices and found deficiencies, they then had an obligation to support the people at the plants in addressing any deficiencies. Their performance was based on the level of improvement in each best practice area, and the production and financial results thereto. So, how did this play out at the plants?

Morris (Mo) Autonemi, plant manager of BM's Independence plant, was reviewing a new product they were about to take on, when he was interrupted by one of his production managers, Ott Knot. "What's this new initiative?" Ott asked.

"Oh, another environmental exercise. We had one of our plants have a significant release last month, because of a failed valve, or an operator not operating the valve properly, and they were fined, and the response is for corporate to do an audit, and then respond to the audit," responded Mo.

"Seems like we have an audit every time we get a boo-boo," replied Ott.

"Yes, I know, but let's not make a big deal of this. Look at this as another opportunity to get better.   I'd like you to check to see if we have similar or identical valves as the one in question – here," as he handed a spec sheet to Ott, "And make sure these valves are in proper working order, and that our people are trained in how to operate them. Have that done by the end of the month."

"Ok, no biggie," Ott replied and then left.

This was a routine thing for Mo, but he handled it with aplomb, never getting too excited about the next audit or review, but rather, focusing on getting the right people in the right jobs, and making sure they had the right tools and training to do that job. He routinely called upon corporate to provide any additional resource to address a particularly issue, whether it be safety, environmental, or operational. Over the years, he had found that if everyone did the basics really well in the way the plant is operated and maintained, which is how he thought of best practices, then everything else would take care of itself.

And, even knowing that he had some leeway in getting additional resources and capital, he would routinely challenge his people to make do with what they had first, but if they had a good case for the additional resource, would provide it. But, he was not tolerant of people not doing the basics well.

Results at Independence were quite good. Gross profits increased year on year for four years running, along with quality, on-time delivery, and, safety.

Less operational autonomy, fewer initiatives, and more financial autonomy seemed to be working better than its opposite.

The Lessons: 1) Initiative overload will assure you do several things poorly. Limit them to about three, fewer if each is large in scope. 2) If you're going to launch an initiative, make sure it's adequately resourced, at both corporate and plant levels. 3) Give plants more financial autonomy, and less operational autonomy in their practices, but only after working with them in defining and adequately resourcing the practices you expect them to apply.

Part III

Related to
A Few Popular Tools

5S, or Is It 4S?

1

"Hey, did you hear?" asked Neely Dunn, a maintenance supervisor at Cannawinya.

"Hear what?" answered Neera Nuff, his close cousin.

"Old 'Rustybutt' is startin' *another* initiative," Neely replied, cynicism oozing in his voice as he emphasized the word *another*. The manager, Rusty Buttinsky, at his staff meeting that morning had announced that they were going to start a 5S program – sort, straighten, scrub, systematize and standardize. This was one of the more common translations for 5S, a Japanese method for improvement. It was actually an abbreviation for seiri, seiton, seiso, seiketsu, shitsuke, and depending on who did the translation, you could end up with variations on exactly what it meant. In any event, old 'Rustybutt', as he was affectionately, or un-affectionately, known, was at it again. He loved initiatives, having started a couple a year over the past two years. Unfortunately, the initiatives were just that, and didn't seem to have much staying power.

Neera thought aloud, "I reckon he's going to keep trying them until he gets one that sticks."

"Uh huh," agreed Neely, as he shook his head in disbelief.

Soon thereafter, Neely and Neera's boss, Herwe Goagin, called a meeting.

"We've been selected to do the pilot for the new 5S program," Herwe announced. Moans rumbled through the room.

To which Herwe said firmly, "Yeah, I know, but we're going to do this, so get over it."

"Selected, or volunteered, or instructed?" Neera whispered among the moans, "He's always doin' this. Why do we have to be the first one in, *every time*?"

Herwe continued, "As you know, housekeeping around here isn't nearly as good as it should be."

"Yeah, he's keep reminding us. I wonder how his house looks. Probably not much different than his nasty car," Neely whispered back at Neera.

Herwe went on, "So we're going to finally get it right using the 5S program – sort, straighten, scrub, systematize and standardize. I need five volunteers to work with me on the preening area." Pausing, "Neely and Neera, was that you volunteering a minute ago. I couldn't hear exactly what you said, but it seemed to have some enthusiasm in it."

"Uhhhhhhhhh," Neely stammered, looking trapped and confused.

But before he could say anything, Herwe quickly went on, "Thanks for volunteering. I really appreciate your help."

"Crap," Neely whispered under his breath.

Herwe eventually got the volunteers needed, and then told "the team" as he called it "Let's start on this bright and early Monday morning. We can probably knock this off in a day."

Monday morning everyone showed up, with "bells on" so to speak.

Herwe, who had been to a one day training course on 5S, began with some suggestions, "OK, the first thing we're going to do is sort. Anything you don't need in the next two weeks goes into the stock room or tool crib." And so it began.

When they began to bring 'stuff' to the stock room, the storeman on duty, Wally Maart, was not happy, "What am I supposed to do with this crap? I don't have a place for this. My boss just chewed my butt because of our inventory being too high, and now you bring more. He said he was going to take away some of my space for warehousing some of our product. What's this 'stuff' worth anyway, so I can do an accounting, IF we decide to take it?" emphasizing the IF.

"How should we know," Neely answered, "We were just told to bring it here. Put it in for whatever you think it's worth."

"Nothing's being put in for more than a dollar, IF we decide to go ahead," Wally responded, again putting a lot of emphasis on the IF. He picked up the phone to call his boss, the manager of purchasing. "Hey boss, Herwe wants us to re-stock a bunch of stuff they're taking out of the preening area. Says they're doing a 5S thing, whatever that is, and need to clear out some stuff from there."

Neely could hear the "Bullcrap!" from where he was standing, and took a deep breath. He didn't really want to take all this stuff back to the area.

Neely intervened, "Could you ask him to call Herwe and resolve this? I'll let Herwe know. In the meantime, can we leave this stuff here?"

Wally frowned, and finally relented, "OK, but if my boss doesn't agree to it, do you promise to come get it and take it back?"

"Promise," said Neely, only half-heartedly. He really didn't want to drag all this stuff back. You could almost see his fingers crossed behind his back.

It took until noon to resolve the issue, with Rusty Buttinsky finally having to get involved. Remember the 5S effort is in fact Old Rustybutt's initiative, and he finally just told Wally he was going to take the stuff into the storeroom, in spite of the fact that purchasing didn't report to him. It had been centralized back at corporate. But, he did control the site and all its facilities. Wally wasn't happy, nor was his boss, since one of their KPI's was inventory management with higher levels lowering their performance review. But, that's another story.

By the end of the day, the 5S team had in fact sorted all the stuff, and left most of it at the door of a very disgruntled Wally for stocking. He still wanted part numbers and stock names, something no one had considered before, and Neera was assigned to do this, in the next week or so.

Unfortunately, they hadn't done any of the 'straighten' or 'scrub', let alone the 'systematize' and 'standardize.' So much for getting 5S done in one day.

Herwe looked frustrated, "Well, let's continue tomorrow."

"Wait," the team members chimed almost in unison. Neely continued, "We've only got the one day set aside for this. What about the maintenance and production work we've scheduled for tomorrow? I'm supposed to install the new drive motor on the conveyor, and Neera here is part of the startup team. I don't know what everyone else had planned." The others nodded, and began mumbling about what they had planned.

"Well, just be here. Give me a list of what you've got lined up," Herwe quietly demanded, "I'll take care of it."

"Maybe we should think about the next two or three days, considering the progress we've *not* made today," Neely suggested, highlighting *not*.

"OK, OK, so we didn't make our schedule. I'll handle it. I want this done," Herwe emphasized. He wasn't about to let the latest initiative fail.

So, the next day everyone showed up and began to straighten – actually doing a little so-called process mapping to see where things needed to be to best support the work being done. They even painted and labeled a few boxes for places to put things, and made up one small shadow board. Neely noted that Wally wasn't very enthusiastic about getting them the paint and materials for the work, but he finally got it to them.

They began scrubbing toward the end of the day, but clearly it was going to take at least another day, which Herwe said he would handle. As they scrubbed, it was clear that some things needed repairs, mostly simple things, like tightening and straightening, but one component needed a complete replacement.

Herwe wrote up an urgent work order for that and tagged it out. He noted that it even looked dangerous to operate in its current condition, since the protective guards were just barely hanging on. And, most of the gear needed a good coat of paint, so that had to be done as well. Wally continued to begrudgingly support them. Meanwhile the work the five team members had planned for the week was being delayed.

Finally, near the end of the fourth day, the work was finished, at least the sort, straighten, scrub part of the 5S program.

Herwe called everyone together to congratulate them on a job well done. And, in fact the preening area did look pretty good. And they had found any number of defects, some pretty serious from an operational or safety view, and some not so much so. Everyone was pretty proud of how the place looked, even Herwe.

"Hey Herwe," Neely teased, "Maybe you could have us work on that old jalopy you drive. We could turn it into a polished antique!"

"Just never you mind," Herwe replied, slightly offended.

"What about the 'systematize and standardize' part?" asked Neera, "I thought we were supposed to do something with that too."

"Just keep things this way," Herwe shot back. "That's the system we're going to use, just keep it this way," he repeated. "Besides, you need to get back to work."

"Oh yeah, there is that," Neely replied, "Any overtime allowed for us to catch up?"

"You know that overtime has been suspended, so why are you asking," Herwe glared.

"Just asking," Neely said, "You could've just said no."

In truth, Herwe didn't really understand what systematize meant.

Neely advised him that systematize meant things like setting up a schedule for reviewing the area and looking for even more ways to make it better, and setting aside the time to do that; and standardize meant things like having a checklist or two that would be used by the people in the area to keep it in good condition, and even make it better.

Herwe didn't understand either that 5S was not about housekeeping – that was a consequence. It was really about defect detection and elimination, error proofing, and workplace discipline. Housekeeping came as a result of that.

Six months later, because they hadn't systematized and standardized, the area was pretty much back to where it had been before the exercise. Herwe had done what most people, that is 4S – sort, straighten, scrub, and STOP. And so, things deteriorate back to where they were unless you have a process to sustaining the changes.

Incidentally, because of the delays in getting the other work done, they nearly missed delivery on a major order. It was only saved when 'Old Rustybutt' stepped in and authorized the overtime to catch up. After all, it was his initiative that had impacted the delivery in the first place.

The Lessons: 1) Most folks do 4S – sort, straighten, scrub, and **stop**. If that's your view, don't bother. 2) Do all five S's, including systematize and standardize, so you can sustain. It's a "forever thing". 3) Keep in mind that the purpose of 5S is defect detection and elimination, error proofing, and workplace discipline, not housekeeping. Housekeeping is a consequence.

Lean and Mean, or Skinny and Ticked?

2

Lean Manufacturing was first described by Jim Womac in his assessment of the Toyota Production System. Since then, untold books have been written about being lean, and untold consultants have made many a fortune working with people to become lean, apparently with little success. The story below illustrates some of the pitfalls of applying lean principles.

After years of cost cutting, Kidencaboodle Company was still in the doldrums relative to performance. In fact, saying their performance as "in the doldrums" was being kind. More accurately, they were in deep doodoo.

The new COO, Lance Alott, had been hired to turn things around, and indeed had a track record for that. If you looked at his resume over the past 10-15 years, he had turned around four companies, staying at each one for something over three years.

Before joining Kidencaboodle, and between jobs, Lance had recently attended a week-long intensive seminar on lean manufacturing, concluding that this business strategy fit perfectly with his skills and experience. Lean companies had lower inventories, lower costs, high quality, and excellent delivery performance. Lance believed that he had done just that in all his previous companies, particularly with regard to lower inventories and costs.

Sadly, Lance hadn't walked around the company's plants to see for himself the state of the assets. It was appalling.

But never mind that, we're getting ahead of ourselves.

Meanwhile, down in Joondalup plant, one that was typical of the entire operation, things weren't going well. Years of cost cutting to make the plant more profitable had only made things worse – the assets were in bad condition, having had maintenance budgets cut year on year.

Stony Lonesome, the maintenance manager, was a somber, lonely guy, who always had a stern look on his face. Maybe this was because he was totally exasperated. He only had one more year before he was eligible to retire, and couldn't wait to get there.

His counterpart in production, Sue Perintendent, was equally frustrated, having had her operating staff cut several times over the past few years. She was barely able to make her production plans.

Of course, the plant manager, Mani Festing, wasn't faring any better, but he was working hard to "toe the company line". He called Sue and Stony together to make a major announcement. The new COO, Lance Alott, had decreed that they were going to apply lean manufacturing principles, effective immediately.

Mani read a memo from Lance regarding the new lean manufacturing initiative. Inventory – finished goods, work-in-process, raw material *and* spare parts – all had to be reduced. Moreover, costs had to be reduced, and quality and delivery had to improve. All at the same time. Lance was driven to make lean the foundation of this turnaround.

"What?! He thinks he can just ride in on his white horse and make us lean," howled Sue, "Lean is a long term, cultural thing."

Stony piled on, "We've been cutting inventory, and costs, for years now, and what have we gotten? Look around you! We're in the crapper, and nobody seems to notice." He looked squarely into Mani's eyes, as if his statement was an indictment.

"Besides," he continued, "From what I've read about lean, its foundation is long term thinking, even at the risk of short term profits, process mapping, and employee engagement. That's hard enough to do, but the next level is process stability and equipment reliability. We don't have anything like that."

Without missing a beat, Sue jumped in before Mani could even offer any rebuttal, "Inventory is a counter measure for un-reliability and process in-stability. If we reduce inventory, we'll even further jeopardize our performance – it'll get worse."

Stony jumped in about this point, "Yeah, lean means fit and capable, like an athlete. Your version of lean means skinny, and pissed off." A silence came upon the room.

With a pause in the discussion, Mani saw his opportunity, "You finished?"

Without waiting for an answer, he continued, "We don't really have any choice. From what I hear, anybody that goes contrary to Lance will be quickly removed. I've called some friends at a couple of his former plants. That's the word I get. Either of you ready to retire early?"

Sue and Stony hung their heads, recognizing the dilemma they were facing. "Only one year to go," thought Stony, "Surely I can put up with this for another year."

And so it went. Manufacturing and parts inventories were reduced another 10%, and downtime went up because of the unavailability of parts, and then on-time-delivery deteriorated because of unavailability of machinery, or feedstock from the upstream area. And, costs stayed about the same, which means gross profit stayed about the same – poor!

Of course, Lance was a very unhappy person. In spite of his "leadership", the company didn't seem to be getting any better. His approach had always worked before – make 'em sweat, cut their resources, and they'll figure it out, and make him a hero.

What Lance didn't realize was that his approach had already been used, twice. It tends to work for three or four years, but after that, all you're doing is driving the business into the ground, a death spiral. Lance's timing in this business wasn't very good.

In fact, his approach took the operation from skinny and ticked to anorexic. A year after his arrival, he was sent packing, but not before the company announced the sale of the business to a group of venture capitalists. Maybe they could breathe new life into it?

Stony retired with full benefits.

The Lesson: 1) The foundation of lean manufacturing is long term thinking, process mapping, and employee engagement in improvement, along with process stability and equipment reliability. Attempting to be "lean" without laying the foundational elements is folly.

TPM –
Totally Painted Machines?

3

"Doozy's at it again," moaned Hada Nuff, a mechanic, referring to his boss, Willie Duzitrite.

"What is it this time?" Closa Nuff, his brother, quizzed, sensing another program inspired by yet another consultant passing through Mildewa Company.

"Well, you remember that 5S thing that we went through last year?" Hada asked.

"Uh huh, the one where we did the initial cleaning, and not much else," responded Closa grumpily, "Place looked like a dump again five months later."

"That's the one," Hada responded before Closa could say anything more. "Well this time we're going to do TPM. Woo Woo!", as he feigned joy in yet another program.

"What's TPM? Totally Painted Machines," Closa said sarcastically. "No wait, the M has to stand for maintenance, that's the only thing he knows, or has any authority over. Or, wait, how 'bout totally pooped maintainers. That's how I feel right now."

"Well you're right about the maintenance thing, but wrong about totally pooped," Hada said. "TPM stands for Total Productive Maintenance."

"Huh? So, we're supposed to be totally productive, while the guys in operations just lay back and watch us work," Closa was getting a little antsy about this TPM thing.

"Sure sounds like it, but Doozy says not to get my tighty whiteys in a knot. He's called a meeting tomorrow morning to talk to us about it," pleaded Hada, "We need to be there."

Taking a long, deep breath, "OK, here we go again," Closa sighed.

So, the next morning, there's Doozy, along with Hada, Closa, and all the rest of Doozy's staff. Having been through this before, most of the people are less than enthusiastic, but the attitude seems to be "What the heck, even a blind hog can find an acorn every now and again. Maybe this time Doozy's bright idea will work." One of the guys even said that, but not so that Doozy could hear it.

Doozy began outlining the basic concepts of TPM, or Total Productive Maintenance.

"TPM is about maintaining plant and equipment function, not just fixing things," Doozy began.

He barely got the words out of his mouth when Closa interrupted, "Anybody tell that to operations or design? All we do is fix things, all they seem to do is break'em. We can't fix'em faster than they can break'em."

"Stay with me. I'll get to that issue in just a minute," Doozy cut him off, and continued, "Another fundamental principle of TPM is that when equipment is new, it is a bad as it will ever be. We're going to constantly improve it."

Hada jumped in this time, "Well there ought to be plenty of opportunity to do that. Have you seen the crap that the new project just delivered? It'll be another three months before we get that thing working right."

Taking a deep breath, Hada continued, "We've already spent $100,000 in maintenance to get it going, and we haven't even begun to think about the spares we need for that thing. Apparently spares weren't part of the project budget. And, none of what we've spent on it is in our budget."

Doozy held up his hand and also took a deep breath, "Let's go on. TPM calls for measuring Overall Equipment Effectiveness or OEE, that is, you measure all production losses that deviate from ideal – rate losses, quality losses, and availability losses – anything that's less than perfection. You're supposed to measure it and then manage it, involving the shop floor in minimizing the losses."

Closa played tag team well with Hada, so he jumped in this time, "It's about time you got to involving production. They hold our feet to the fire on availability when we're doing maintenance – 'we need it back, we need it back, *now*' is their favorite saying. Nobody seems to care much when they're not running because of changeovers, or production planning screw-ups, or shift handover, or scrap and rework problems, or raw material problems, or…" His voice drifted off.

"Well, if we measure the production losses, it'll give us a better handle on where to focus our time, won't it?" asked Doozy.

"Has Dunn Thet agreed to do this?" referring to the operations manager, Hada was suspicious of the whole thing.

"No, not yet, we're meeting tomorrow to discuss the possibility of using this approach," responded Doozy.

"Good luck with that," Closa said sharply, "He doesn't like to see any numbers that make him look bad. And this OEE thing might make everyone look bad.

"We'll see," Doozy continued. This was harder than he thought it was going to be. "TPM calls for restoring equipment performance to like-new, or better."

Hada jumps in again, "Boy you just keep diggin' this hole deeper don't you. You know, when you're in a hole, you should stop diggin'. We've been patching about half the equipment out there for years – remember operations is always demanding 'we want it back *now*'? And now all of a sudden we're goin' to make things like-new, *or better*. Who's goin' to turn the switch and make that light come on?" The sarcasm was flowing.

He knew the cynicism was partly deserved, but Doozy continued, "TPM calls for operator care and involvement in maintaining the equipment."

"Now that's a good one," Closa laughed this time, "When was the last time you saw that? I thought I just said to stop diggin'."

Doozy ignored him this time, "TPM calls for training and developing employee skills."

"It just keeps gettin' better doesn't it?" Hada looked at Closa, "The last time I had any training in anything other than safety and admin stuff was two years ago. I had to learn that new alignment system by trial and error, mostly error the first two or three times. Go on," Hada stared at Doozy.

Doozy was getting a little exasperated, but he trooped on, "TPM calls for maintenance prevention, and equipment management, *in the design*."

"Closa interrupted yet again, "I think we talked about that just a minute ago, didn't we? That new project that we're having so much trouble getting up and running. I don't think the project guys know much about this part of TPM."

"Granted," Doozy replied, "But we've got to start somewhere."

"And finally," Doozy was really glad to get to the last point, "TPM calls for the effective use of planned, preventive and predictive maintenance, making the work more efficient, and effective."

"Ta dah! At last something that we have some control over," Hada applauded.

Doozy decided to let things sit for a moment for people to reflect on what he'd just struggled to get through. It all seemed to make so much sense, but now that he'd been through this with his staff, he saw that this was going to be a very difficult process to get in place.

He thought to himself, "These were the guys that worked for him, and their enthusiasm was less than what he'd hoped for. How was he going to convince the operations and design people to buy into all this?"

After a moment, Hada looked a little puzzled and had a more serious tone, "Doozy, most of this looks like it relates to operations, design, HR, IT - people other than us. Yeah, we have the maintenance piece, but most of this is controlled by those folks. Why is it called Total Productive Maintenance? Why not Total Productive Manufacturing, if you want to keep the TPM label? It ought to sell better that way." Hada did have a little thoughtfulness in him after all.

"Good point," responded Doozy, "In fact I've read that it should have been called that, but that was after the book on TPM was published. We can call it whatever we want."

"Well you better. As soon as Pud Fudder (the senior operations supervisor) and Dunn Thet see the word maintenance, they're going to glaze over and go somewhere else," Closa suggested.

"OK, we'll do that," agreed Doozy, "I'll change all the slides to reflect that."

"Oh, by the way, Ben Thur is coming back," Doozy surprised everyone, "It seems that senior management hasn't been too happy with his replacement, old Rufenuf, (Rob Ruffenufton) so Ben's coming back to get things back on track. He'll be here in two weeks, so maybe I should wait til then to start the discussion with him and Dunn."

"Oh joy, I can hardly wait," Hada said, somewhat sarcastically. Doozy wasn't sure if Hada was referring to Doozy coming back or getting around to doing the presentation, but he didn't pursue it, seeing little value in asking for more sarcasm.

"Me too," echoed Closa, "I'm so happy I could just wet myself." Doozy rolled his eyes and left.

Two weeks passed, but without Doozy being able to review all this with Dunn or Pud. They were just too busy, it seemed.

Ben Thur arrived and most seemed to be glad about his return, except maybe for Dunn Thet, who thought he should have been promoted into the job. Rufenuf had really mucked things up in his view, and he thought he deserved the chance to get them back on track. Ben wasn't aggressive enough.

Anyway, it took Doozy a week to get a couple hours scheduled for Ben and Dunn to meet with him on TPM. Ben was familiar with the people and production process and would ramp up pretty quickly, but wanted to get a clearer picture of how things may have changed, and the current condition of the plant. And, Doozy wanted Dunn there as well.

Finally, Doozy began his presentation regarding TPM, "I'd like to go over an improvement method called Total Productive Manufacturing, or TPM, and see if you think this would work for us."

As soon as the words were out of his mouth, Ben interrupted, "Seems like we did a thing on 5S or something like that just before I left, and we only budgeted enough to do one project. Did that ever go anywhere? More importantly, is this another one of those, where we churn the pot, but don't get any butter?" Ben had grown up on a dairy farm.

"No, I wanted to get everybody agreeing to at least try this in one area before we spend a lot of money on it, but then don't sustain it, " responded Doozy.

"Go on," Ben was obviously a little skeptical.

Doozy began outlining the basic concepts of TPM, or Total Productive Manufacturing, specifically avoiding using the word maintenance.

"TPM is about maintaining plant and equipment function, not just fixing things," he opened.

Dunn jumped in, "So do you want to stop fixing things?"

"No, that's part of my job, but it would make my life easier, and save us some money, if I had to fix fewer things. Maybe if we could work together to solve some of these problems, both our lives would be easier." He said calmly, trying not to provoke Dunn, who simply nodded, still seeming skeptical.

"Another fundamental principle of TPM is that when equipment is new, it is a bad as it will ever be. We're going to constantly improve it."

Dunn said nearly the same things as Hada had said a few days before, "Well that new project we just took over is just about as bad as it will ever be, isn't it? It's gonna be months before we get that thing working right." Dunn wasn't aware of the $100,000 in extra maintenance costs already incurred, but he was more agreeable to doing a better job with projects so that the startup phase was much easier.

Doozy, continued, "TPM calls for measuring Overall Equipment Effectiveness or OEE, that is, you measure all production losses that deviate from ideal – rate losses, quality losses, and availability losses – anything that's less than perfection. You're supposed to measure it and then manage it, involving the shop floor in minimizing the losses."

Dunn was more suspicious at this point, "We already measure rates, and quality, and downtime. Is this new?"

Doozy quickly countered, "But this puts it all together into a single number for how well we're doing. And, right now, we don't count the production losses during product changes, *or* any time we can get back on line within 15 minutes or less, *or* any production delays because of sales trying to change our production schedule. There are a lot of opportunities for improving our production capability out there. I did a rough calculation which said we're about 55% of ideal."

At this, Dunn countered as well, seeming irritated, "Our utilization is 92%, or better, and that's pretty good." Recall that Dunn liked to look good, especially in front of his boss.

Doozy responded, "Yeah, but that only counts the time that you're producing according to the production plan, no matter what rate you're at, and it doesn't count all the things I just mentioned. When you take those into account, we're probably in the 50-60% range. Let's look at a calculation I did from some information I got from Bo, your senior operations supervisor on Line No. 1. The ideal rate is 100 units per hour. We've shown we can do that. So in a 12 hour period we should be able to make 1,200 units. But, last month we only produced 550 on average." Showing an example calculation he continued, "When we take into account all the losses from rate, quality/scrap, downtime, changeovers, production plan changes, and so on, we only do about 55% of ideal. I'm told that's about average, for this kind of process, and that world class is in the 80-85% range."

Dunn was not pleased at looking average in front of Ben, and had been touting the 92-95% numbers for years, "I'll need to look at this and let you know. Just so you know how I feel right now, I don't agree with this."

Doozy remained calm, expecting something like this, "That's fine. I'll be glad to take you through some of the details I've dug up, but feel free to go over it with Bo." Doozy handed Dunn the data and preliminary analysis, and continued, "The way I see it, if we measure **ALL** the production losses, and then figure out which ones will be easiest to address, it'll give us a better handle on where to focus our time, won't it?"

Dunn, who couldn't really disagree at this point, just mumbled "No. I'll have a look at this."

Meanwhile, Ben was just listening thoughtfully.

Doozy continued. This was going better than he thought, especially after the harangue he went through with Hada and Closa, "TPM calls for restoring equipment performance to like-new, *or better*. One thing I need your help with Dunn is that we've been patching about half the equipment out there for years. I know there's always a sense of urgency about getting equipment back on line, and we hear 'we want it back *now*' a lot, but there are times when we really need to take the time to do things right, as in 'like new or better'."

Ben jumped in on this one. "Doozy, I want you to adopt this approach from now on, but I want you to make sure you do the work as quickly as possible, while getting the job done as well as possible. Dunn I want you to make sure he has the time to do things right. If either one of you sees a problem with this approach, for example, it affects delivery to a customer, then you come and talk to me about it." Looking at Dunn, "Besides, you don't want Doozy to do poor work do you?"

"I just want things back quickly," Dunn retorted, "You're going to be on my case when we don't make delivery."

"Let's try this, and we'll talk more at the staff meetings about getting the balance right," Ben ended the discussion on this point.

Doozy continued, "TPM calls for operator care and involvement in maintaining the equipment."

"So, you want us to do your job," Dunn seemed a little hostile about this one.

"No, no," responded Doozy defensively. "But I would like the operators to take better care of the equipment, and maybe do some simple things – TLC, tender, loving care, or tighten, lubricate and clean. I've seen them write work orders for us to come and tighten a panel screw or a loose nut on a flange, something they could have easily done, particularly when we're understaffed, and always have several big jobs lined up."

Before Dunn could interrupt, Doozy barely caught his breath and went on, "And the equipment is really dirty when we come to maintain it. Dirt is the enemy of reliability you know. Cleanliness is next to godliness?" He finally paused, and added sheepishly, "Sorry, I didn't really mean to get up on my soapbox, but I'd just like some help from you and your guys in keeping things running. My mother said 'take care of the place where you make your living, so it will take care of you.' I'd like to see us work together to do that."

Dunn had been getting irritated, but those last few comments helped him to calm down. "So what do you want me to do?"

Doozy looked plaintively, "Well if you'd get your guys to keep the equipment clean, that would make our lives easier when we do maintenance, and it might even stop a few failures. Ask them to tighten the things they can easily do. I know some of them are going to balk because of so-called union contract issues, but I've read the contract and it provides for operators to do both these things. We should start applying the contract for things that we can do as quickly as some of them like to apply it to things they can't do. These would make a good start."

Dunn was about to say something, when Ben cut him off, "These seem like reasonable things to me. Does the contract really allow operators to do minor maintenance, TLC, stuff?"

Doozy, had the contract with him, and that particular page marked, showing it to Ben and Dunn. "So, why haven't we been doing these things Dunn?" Ben asked.

Dunn responded with a blank stare, and then said, blowing out a deep breath, "I don't know. Habit of all the years of not doing it I suppose."

Ben took it from there, "Well we need to get on it, and do these simple things for a start. I'll meet with you and your supervisors to get the discussion going. We won't present it as a ultimatum, but as more of a question, but making it clear we expect folks to do this, and then we'll meet with each of the area team operators and make the case again, asking them what they think it means, and how we might be able to do these things, or what might stop us. We'll handle the blockers on the spot, or get back to them quickly with an answer or a plan. But, we'll make it clear that these are things we expect."

"OK, Boss," Dunn gave up on changing anyone's mind.

Doozy went on, "TPM calls for training and developing employee skills."

They nodded their head in agreement on this point, but Doozy quipped first, "My guys say the last time they had any training in anything other than safety and admin stuff was two years ago, just before you left Ben. For example, they had to learn that new alignment system by trial and error, mostly error the first two or three times they used it."

Ben was getting into all this and picked up the phone and called his HR manager, Bea Nicely. "Hey, this is Ben, how many hours, on average, does each person get in skills development training? Don't count safety and admin stuff."

"Uhhh, we don't separate them like that," Bea said, somewhat confused.

"Well break it out for me in terms of total training hours per year, average per person, and then break the total into categories for safety, admin, and skills development," Ben demanded.

"Well, hang on a minute," as Bea shuffled papers and clicked on her computer. "Looks like an average of about 30 hours per year total."

"Thanks, would you get me the breakdown tomorrow?" although it wasn't really a question, rather more of a demand.

"OK," Bea responded a bit heavily. More work tonight.

"I'll have a look at this and we'll get together in the next week or so to review this issue," Ben thought out loud, "You two put together, or maybe pull out your old training plans, and let's see if we can get a better handle on this. You know we spend millions each year maintaining and improving our equipment, and apparently damn little maintaining and improving our people and their skills. That has to change." Ben looked at Doozy to continue.

Doozy trooped on, "TPM calls for maintenance prevention, and equipment management, *in the design.*"

"I think we just discussed that new project that's such a mess," Dunn said, agreeing more enthusiastically with Doozy.

"Granted," Doozy replied, "But we may want to push for this later on."

Ben interjected again "I'd like to start the thinking now, so I'll set up a meeting with projects to talk more strategically, using our experience here to start the discussion."

Ben looked back at Doozy.

"And finally," Doozy was really glad to get to the last point, "TPM calls for the effective use of planned, preventive and predictive maintenance, making the work more efficient, and effective."

"Yeah, finally, something you have to take responsibility for," Dunn sighed.

Doozy said "That's it. Those are the key principles of TPM. We need to decide if we want to use this model, and if so where to start." He was pleased that Ben Thur had been fairly supportive; and Dunn Thet hadn't been as oppositional as he had anticipated.

Ben summarized, "Well I've got a few actions already – talking to the projects guys about involving us more up front in the design of things they do, and looking at our training plan and budget. Dunn and I are going to meet with the Ops supervisors and operators to look at this issue of operator care and TLC." Pausing for effect, he continued, "From now on you two are going to work together to 'restore equipment to like-new, or better'; and you're going to get this OEE measure in place. We're going to measure OEE and understand, and *manage*, all those losses. Dunn you take the lead on OEE. Don't take offense, but I've never believed those utilization numbers anyway. I want a plan for that in the next month. And, Doozy, you're going to get me a plan for how we're going to do PM, and predictive maintenance, and all the planning that goes with it. I'd like that in the next month too."

He paused to catch his breath, "Finally, you're both going to resurrect your training plans and feed that to me for Bea and me to work on the budget. I'm not expecting a polished plan on any of these, but I don't want to put this off til it's polished. I want to get moving. Anyway, that's a pretty good start, don't you think?"

Ben, Doozy, and Dunn went about their efforts in a methodical, pragmatic way, steadied by Ben's reasoned approach to everything. It was a struggle at first, as they tried to get all the initial things done in a month, an impossible task to begin with, but Ben was patient as long as he was seeing reasonable progress being made, and people not being obstinate. When progress wasn't being made, or people were dragging their feet or getting in the way, he quickly stepped in and made his expectations clear. While pragmatic about most things, he wanted to create a sense of urgency in everyone about applying these basic principles.

It turned out that their OEE was in fact 55%, but over the next two years, it increased to 75%, and maintenance costs dropped some 20%. Safety and environmental performance improved as well – things worked better, reducing the risk of these incidents. And quality and on time delivery improved dramatically. Though still not world class, people were working together, aligned to a common purpose under the Total Productive Manufacturing banner, and getting good results.

Ben was promoted the next year and left once again, only this time to try to apply these principles across the entire business.

The Lesson: 1) TPM is far more than maintenance, and should be called Total Productive Manufacturing. 2) Work together to do the right things, and the right things will happen.

RCM – Reliability Centered Misery?

4

After getting pretty good results from their TPM effort, Doozy was looking for the next tool for improvement, and decided that RCM, or reliability centered maintenance, was just the thing.

"Here we go again," remarked Hada Nuff, "Doozy's called another meeting to talk about reliability centered maintenance. He calls it RCM, but it feels like reliability centered misery." You remember - Doozy is Willie Duzitrite, Hada's boss.

"Oh man," exclaimed Closa Nuff, his brother and workmate, "Those things are so boring, sitting around all day long, talking about what might happen, and how things might go wrong. There must be a bazillion ways that things can go wrong. Do we have to talk about every one of them?"

"Apparently, we do," Hada replied in a resigned tone, "But, I think we should just focus on the ones that actually *have* gone wrong. That seems more practical to me. Why can't we just do 'hillbilly RCM' (something he had picked up from a friend from Eastern Kentucky), that is, asking four simple questions and acting on them – What's the system supposed to do? What's stopping it from doing that? What's hurtin' us the most? And, finally what are we goin' to do about the things that are hurtin' us the most? We seem to be spendin' more time analyzin' things that might never happen than we do solving the things that do."

Clearly he was frustrated, "We've been at this now for five days, with no end in sight. RCM feels more like a resource consuming monster. Besides, I've got all these other jobs piling up. Who's supposed to be doin' them?"

"Doozy said it was only one day a week til we get done, so I reckon we're supposed to work harder during the other four days a week. I just hope that's not a sneaky way to show that we're not being as productive as we could," Closa worried. He was indeed a worry-wart, always fretting about one thing or another. He reminded Hada of his grandmother who was always commiserating with whoever would listen.

"This will make the fourth day of 'analysis', but the operating people haven't shown up since the first day," complained Hada, "Mani Pulate, the senior operations supervisor, told me this was about reliability centered **maintenance**, and he put a lot of emphasis on **maintenance**, and hasn't been back since. He said he didn't see the point in his people coming to all these maintenance meetings. I don't know how we're supposed to stop all the failures by ourselves, when they won't start things up right, won't shut things down right, and won't operate'em right. Seems pretty futile to me. I tried to make that point to him, but he wasn't in the mood to listen to me whining."

They labored on, and grew to know first-hand why RCM was sometimes called reliability centered misery. Another three weeks passed, and Doozy was finally ready to present his findings and recommendations to the senior managers. They had identified most all the ways that things could fail, and how to stop them failing by taking certain actions in the way equipment is operated, designed, or maintained, and how to detect developing problems early with condition monitoring, so you could minimize the impact of the pending failure.

In some cases they actually thought they should stop doing certain things, because those things didn't help avoid problems or detect problems early. Those really were a waste of time and money.

Doozy was really proud of all the work they'd done. The truth be known, Closa and Hada were also pleased with the result, in spite of all the laborious tedium they had experienced. "Finally, we should get to go do something with all this," Closa speculated.

The meeting was attended by Dan Gling, the new plant manager, Dunn Thet, still the operations manager, Mani Pulate, Bea Nicely, the HR/Training manager, and of course, Doozy.

Doozy began his presentation with an overview of RCM, that is, understanding functional requirements, analyzing failure modes, and consequences, and then taking action to minimize the failure modes that had the highest risk and consequence. Much of this was a judgment call, and there was some discussion about the criteria around risk and consequence, but the discussion went pretty well.

Then Doozy got to the heart of the actions. Operators needed to do several tasks, which amounted to about 60% of the changes in tasks, procedures and checklists; maintenance needed to do several other things, which amounted to about 30% of the tasks; and about 10% required some sort of design modification, since the way things were operated had changed. Things began to go downhill at this point.

Dunn and Mani jumped in immediately, with Mani, mostly deferring to Dunn, "Who says we need to do this? How do you know? You're not an operator. We didn't approve this."

"Yeah," Mani chimed in.

Doozy responded defensively, "Well this is what we came up with. You left after day one, so don't be too quick to criticize."

Mani elevated the tone, "This is a maintenance thing. You can't make decisions for operations. I just want the equipment to run right. Look at that, you're saying operations is causing twice as many failures as maintenance. That's just bull crap."

"Yeah," Dunn echoed.

Before Mani could go on, Doozy interrupted, "Well then you should run it right, so we don't have to fix it all the time. Most of the failures are because you *don't* run it right."

"We don't run it right, eh?" quipped Mani, "What about that motor you put in last week with the terminals on backward? It took two or three hours to figure out your dumb mistake, not counting all the startup and shutdown time on either end."

"Yeah, well what about that pump the motor was driving that you ran dry for an hour, before it all finally went up in smoke. You could've hurt somebody on that one. We're just lucky it didn't," Doozy angrily replied.

Things were getting a little out of hand, when Dan interrupted, "All rights guys, calm down. Can we agree there's plenty of opportunity to go around about how we do things better? Doozy, a lot of these things look like they're going to require a lot of resources and cost a lot of money – design changes are expensive, operating procedures and checklists take a lot of time, probably overtime in this case, since our plate is so full already.

He continued, "Likewise for maintenance changes. How much is all that going to cost? We've already spent about $50,000 on the analysis, including that consulting company's time."

Doozy took a deep breath, "Well, we reckon about $200,000, but…"

Before he could finish, Dan interrupted again, clearly perturbed, "$200,000! We don't have that kind of money in our budget. I thought this was going to be a $50,000 project and we were going to see all these improvements, and *save* money. Now you tell me we need another $200,000? That makes this a $250,000 project. I would never have approved this if I'd know this up front."

Thereupon a long quiet pause ensued.

Doozy continued sheepishly, "the 'but' part of my earlier comment was that the $200,000 doesn't include the design changes. We reckon those will be another $250,000."

"Now we're up to a half million?" Dan could hardly believe his ears, "And this is supposed to *save* money?" Dan's tone was more demanding now.

Doozy, now wanted to crawl under the table, but he trooped on, "It *will* save money, about two million in net cost reduction and increased production output, but it will take about two years to get it. I hadn't gotten to that part yet. We need time to make the changes and see the results."

Dan cut him off, emphasizing, "We **DON'T** have the money Doozy. We just *don't*."

"Now what?" asked Doozy.

Another long quiet pause ensued. Dan looked at Doozy, but glanced in Dunn and Mani's direction.

Dan finally said, "Look Doozy, this is good work, in spite of the fact that Mani didn't participate. We've still got plenty of opportunity here to get better. I want you, *and Mani*, to put your heads together and pick the simple things that you and he can do, *together if necessary*. Let's not let what we can't do stop us from doing what we can do."

Continuing, he added, "And Dunn, I want you to support them. We only had $50,000 in the budget for this, not a half million. And we can't get the rest of the money for at least nine months when the next budgeting cycle comes around. So, the costly things will just have to wait."

So, Doozy and Mani left and did in fact do the things they could, both within their groups, and even a couple together. But, later that year, Dan left for another job, and the new manager didn't put much stock in this RCM thing. He placed greater emphasis on other improvement techniques. So, most of the RCM analysis wasted away sitting on a bookshelf.

The Lessons: 1) Before you go into an improvement effort, make sure you've included all the steps of the improvement process, especially the implementation. 2) Make sure all the appropriate parties participate in the analysis and implementation. 3) It helps when you have constancy of purpose by having the same manager in a role more than two years.

Part IV

Particular Anecdotes

The Case of the Gloves[*]   1

One day not too long ago, Gatin C. Nile, a mechanic, was reflecting on all the things he had to do and what little time he had to do them. The company, Naracoot, was on a new "empowerment" kick (the latest in a series of initiatives, or what most folks viewed as yet another program of the month), but he felt less empowered than ever. Further, it seemed to him that the priorities were backwards. He believed that doing the basic, "easy" stuff like tightening, lubricating, and cleaning, such as what he did on his old Jeep, would result in fewer breakdowns. Unfortunately, not many people saw much value, or glamour, in that kind of work. There just weren't too many "kudos" for it – it was pretty dull work; and there was constant pressure to get things done quickly. Besides, with all the breakdowns, he hardly had time for doing the easy stuff – patch and run was his routine mode of operation.

Once he tried to use a "Pre-destruction Authorization" form with the production manager, Payne N. Diaz. That is, he asked Payne to sign a form that said "I hereby authorize premature failure of this equipment because I have not allowed the time for the tasks listed below, which represent precision work." His recollection was that the kerfuffle that followed was more than he wanted to repeat. Old Payne went "ballistic" and wrote him up, though later this was dropped.

So here he was, extremely frustrated, and yet told he was empowered to do better, a real conundrum.

Being a good trooper and wanting to try yet again, he took time to think about what he was really doing for the company, using the new "empowerment" training he had been given.

Reflecting on all this he thought "I'm responsible for eight machines, each with eight positions, with an operator tending each machine. Then it hit him! "How about if I teach the operators to do some of the minor/routine maintenance themselves, especially the kind that requires just a few hand tools?" When he talked with a couple of the operators on shift, they were very receptive. They were really frustrated as well, since when their positions were down, management hounded them, and their work was much more difficult than when the machines and positions were running well.

So, Gatin and two operators gave it some thought and decided that Gatin could train the operators on the afternoon shift to do the minor/routine repairs, and they also decided that no one else would need to know. If they asked the union leadership or the plant management for permission, it would probably get shot down, notwithstanding all the babble about being empowered. So he thought, "If I want to make my job easier and the operators want to make their jobs easier, why not just do it? We're empowered aren't we?"

So, Gatin began preparing. He got several wrenches and screwdrivers from the tool room and some small parts from the shop, and he began to teach the operators how to do the basics to keep their machine positions running product. The operators, with some coaching, quickly were making the minor repairs. Production output nearly doubled. And Gatin was able to get all of his major machine repairs done on time or ahead of time. This allowed him time to help the operators with their maintenance skills and teach them a little more. This empowerment thing was actually working! Life was good.

Until... the inspection department started rejecting more of the product because of grease on the outer layers of the white-coated material they were producing – but only on the afternoon shift.

Payne and one of his supervisors, Mousy, came down to see what was wrong and found that operators were getting grease on their gloves when they did minor repairs, and when they handled the product, it too got greasy. Payne decided that this must stop, and without even considering the 5 Whys approach, he simply issued a decree – "No more maintenance work by operators!"

With that decree, Gatin's workload doubled, so he had no time to continue with the informal training in minor maintenance for the operators. All of his work just couldn't be done on shift. Production volume went down, and was soon back to its original level before they'd done the clandestine training and operator minor maintenance, since more and more positions were not operating while they waited for Gatin or one of his associates. It became pretty gloomy on the afternoon shift. What had been a sterling success (save the rejections), was now becoming very discouraging. Empowerment was on the wane.

But Gatin and the operators on afternoon shift were very resourceful people. They had to be. There weren't many managers and supervisors around then – supervisors and managers did more after-the-fact criticizing, than they did helping solve problems day-to-day. So Gatin and the operators decided to get two pairs of gloves: one for operating and changing product and another for doing the minor repairs. That's all it took. The production levels went back up, and Gatin's repair and restoration work got done on time and to a very high level of quality – he actually had the time for this again.

This sharing of tasks and teamwork contributed to higher levels of productivity and quality for months. Everyone was pleased, even Payne, though he was not aware of the clandestine approach being used by Gatin and his buddies.

Until... someone in the accounting office noticed how much the afternoon shift was spending on gloves. The accounting manager, Beans he was called, came down, looked at the situation, and realized that the operators were each using two pairs of gloves: one for changing product and the other for doing... minor repairs.

"This can't continue," Beans announced, "Besides, don't you remember the production manager saying no more maintenance by operators. Do you want to be written up?" he snorted, "Again?" with an air of arrogance.

Echoing what he'd heard a million times from (the) Payne, he blasted them – "Operators are supposed to operate, and maintenance is supposed to maintain. And besides, look at what has happened to our glove budget."

Gatin didn't think gloves were very expensive, compared to what they were getting in improved production; or that the model of "we break'em, you fix'em" worked very well, but what could he do at that point. He'd already been written up once for this.

To make matters worse, Luke Inferbennies, the union president, got involved at this point, and he was furious when he heard that operators were doing minor repairs. He met with the two "guilty" operators – "What the hell is this with doing maintenance work? That isn't in the contract."

"But, but," protested Con Shuns, one of the operators, "it says right here", pointing to the contract, "that operators are required to do basic care and routine cleaning."

"Dumbass," retorted Luke, "does it say maintenance?"

Con responded quickly and tensely "Well no, the word maintenance isn't in there, but how can you do basic care without doing some minor maintenance? And don't call me dumbass...dumbass!"

Luke took a deep breath and said "Look, the wording is vague on purpose – we want to negotiate what operator care means – that's more money for you, dumb... never mind. You see my point?"

Con eased up a bit, "Yeah, but all we were trying to do was make our lives easier. That's all. And it worked. Now you're dumping crap all over us."

"Well, this has to be negotiated. Period. End of story," fumed Luke quietly. And off he went.

Yes, that was the end of the story, at least for empowerment at this plant. Somehow they never did get back to negotiating the details of operator care. Con and his friend continued to operate; and Gatin continued to struggle along in maintenance as best he could. Burned twice now, he wasn't looking for strike three. Interestingly, the union president never did recognize that jobs are a result of being competitive in the market place, and that making the work more expensive (negotiating for extra money without adding extra value), didn't really make you more competitive.

Sometime later the plant shut down, in spite of Gatin's and the operators' best effort to be empowered, and more productive, and more cost efficient, and more competitive.

The Lesson: The folks doing the work know where the problems are with doing the work, and how to solve them. Management should engage them in doing so.

This story, embellished just a bit, is courtesy of Bob Williamson of Strategic Work Systems, Inc.

The Scarfer Story

2

The Norka steel plant was having all kinds of problems with its so-called scarfer, a rectangular-shaped blow torch that you run large slabs of steel through to burn off the top millimeter of steel to assure the quality of the finished steel slab. It was failing weekly, sometimes more often. Beyond the obvious extra maintenance cost, it was also causing considerable lost production, and while it wasn't working, the entire plant was down, along with operators sitting idly by. What a waste.

Dee Pendible, the new maintenance manager, was racking his brains about this. Work order after work order, and no one seemed to be trying to solve the problem. Being new to the operation, and a bona fide engineer, he was typically focused on root cause analysis and applying engineering methods to solve problems. So, wanting to impress his boss as the new kid on the block with new ideas, he was considering convening a team of people to analyze the scarfer problems using reliability centered maintenance, a process involving the use of failure modes and effects analysis.

Alternatively, maybe he'd do a root cause analysis, to determine what tasks needed to be done to avoid all these failures. In fact, one of the reasons he had been hired was because he was fairly competent in these techniques, having attended several courses, and facilitated a few problems solving sessions himself. Justifiably so, he was pretty proud of this, and wanted to use it here.

In anticipation of this, and being new, he went to Dubb Doofus, one of his engineers to ask who should attend the session, where it should be held, and to get a better understanding of some of the scarfer performance requirements. Doofus had been on a special project for the past six months and so wasn't as familiar with the problems as he might have otherwise been. He was a little rusty, you might say.

Doofus listened politely and patiently to all the questions and suggestions being offered by Dee, his new boss. Finally, he politely interrupted, since that was indeed his nature, "Have you talked to the scarfer operator?"

"No," replied Dee with a quizzical look on his face. Remember Dee liked to apply engineering tools to solve problems. The look on his face said "Why would I do that?"

"You might oughta," Doofus suggested, "before you launch into some fancy-pants analysis."

"Hmmm, maybe you're right," Dee finally responded, both confused and annoyed, not really appreciating Doofus referring to his techniques as 'fancy-pants'.

"Do you have a few minutes now?" Doofus went on.

Clearly this was interrupting Dee's train of thought, and his schedule for the day, but he finally relented, heaving a sigh with "OK, let's do it." They both trudged out to the scarfer.

Doofus began the conversation, introducing Dee to the operator, Ron Ithard and then asking, "We've heard you're having a lot of breakdowns on the scarfer. What do you think the problem is?"

The operator had a surprised look, wondering why someone from maintenance would actually come and talk to him.

Ron thought for a minute, "Well, we've got a lot of problems, but the biggest one is that I get crooked steel from the rolling mill, and it bangs and rubs the scarfer, damages it, and it breaks down a lot more often. Oh yeah, and I've heard the filters on the cooling water for the scarfer plug up a lot, and that heats up the scarfer way beyond its normal operating temperature. Probably makes it easier to damage when it's hot. But hey, I'm just the operator."

"Hmmmm," mulled Dee, "maybe we should go talk to the rolling mill operator to see why the steel he sends here is crooked."

"Good idea," Doofus observed with a smile.

The rolling mill operator, Don Itfast, was surprised as well to see people from maintenance as well, but he observed, "You folks don't get out here much do you, except to fix stuff." He smiled as he welcomed them into his operating cabin. Doofus smiled back, but Dee wasn't sure how to react to this.

Doofus began the conversation again with the comment from the scarfer operator, "Ron, down at the scarfer was just complaining about not getting straight steel from here, and that causes problems, when the steel bumps and rubs the scarfer and damages it. Do you have any ideas about why that's happening?"

Don responded quickly, "Oh, that's easy, when I get the slabs from the ovens, a lot of times they're cold on one side, so when I roll them, they won't roll straight. I've got some latitude in this, but I can't compensate for all the non-uniformity in the temperature."

Clearly, Don understood the problem and was quite articulate about it.

"How often does this happen?" Dee continued with the questioning.

"Every day, most days several times a day," Don advised, "I thought y'all knew this, but were just content with it."

"No, we didn't know," acknowledged Doofus.

They proceeded down to the ovens – large, hot pits with a cover, from which the operators would extract the ingots to be rolled. The first thing they noticed was that the cover was off the top of the pit, but there were no ingots being extracted. Maybe this was a clue? They ambled up to the operator's crane and motioned to him. He wasn't moving any metal, since there appeared to be a short stop on the line for some reason. Maybe the scarfer was down again?

The operator, Bob Kwikli, moved his crane over, got out of the cabin and said "What's up? Who are you guys anyway? Oh, sorry Doofus, I know you. Haven't seen you around in a while."

Doofus replied quickly, almost cutting Bob off, "No, I've been off on a special project for the past six months. Listen, we don't want to take much of your time, so I'll get right to it. The rolling mill operator was just complaining about not getting uniform temperature ingots, and so when he rolls 'em, they go a little crooked on him, and when they get to the scarfer, they sometimes hit it and damage it. Any thoughts on that?"

"Sure, my supervisor told me to leave the tops off the ovens, so I could get ingots in and out more quickly, and improve productivity," Bob responded instantly, "When I do that the ingots on the outside of the ovens cool off on one side. "See," had said, pointing to the obvious.

Dee and Doofus both looked at the ovens, and then at one another, shaking their heads.

"Thanks for your time Bob," Doofus said as they walked away.

Dee, echoed, "Thanks, you've been a big help."

Dee was a little embarrassed, acknowledging, "I see what you mean about not starting with a 'fancy-pants' analysis, and just talking with the folks doing the work. Let go see what we can do about getting the production supervisor to modify his instructions, and let's see if we can verify what Ron said about the filters and get those squared away, maybe with a simple PM. I'm putting the Inspection PM on your list. I'll handle the discussion with the production manager and supervisor to see if we can get the operating instructions changed. Thank you."

The Lesson: 1) Even a Doofus can observe the obvious, so why shouldn't management? 2) Repeated - Talk to the people doing the work if you want to know about the problems with the work.

The Packaging Line Story

3

"Hey, did you hear?" Allus Noital, asked somewhat smugly. Allus was an operations supervisor at Chewbarka's Fido Plant.

"Hear what," responded Hardlee Noes, one of the senior operators.

"We've been acquired, lock, stock and barrel," Allus said proudly, as if she was always in the know, "By that big consumer products company, A&Z."

Hardlee, could hardly contain his disappointment and surprise, "What? I thought the owners were going to keep us private forever, I mean the founders are home town folks who just wanted to make good products. For twenty years, they've always talked about us being one big family."

"Well, maybe $500 million was too big a temptation. Besides, the old man is getting old. Maybe he wanted to cash out before he got **too** old," she said with great emphasis.

"Smart ass," Hardlee was thinking.

"You know what else?" Allus continued without waiting for Hardlee to reply, since he was hardly in the know, "We've been selected for the launch of our products into A&Z's massive marketing and distribution system.

Hardlee never could understand how Allus seemed to be in the know. "Who does she know that I don't," he pondered to himself.

"We've got to make three months' worth of inventory for the launch," she said excitedly.

"Lots of overtime I reckon," thought Hardlee, having been through a campaign or two over the past twenty years.

And indeed it came to pass that Allus was right. A&Z bought them out, and they began the production effort to support the launch. The plant manager, Alice Knervus, a bit of a nerdy person, had tediously run the numbers and they had sufficient production capacity at their bottleneck process to support the launch, but they might need some overtime to make this happen. So she had agreed to the challenge presented by the launch, secretly with the hope that this would put her in a favorable light in the eyes of A&Z's executives, and be a bright spot in her career.

One month later, the situation was disastrous. During the entire month, the line had not met the quota for even one day to support the launch, not one day! And here they were, 30 days into it, with only two weeks of production. And, this was in spite of authorizing any amount of overtime needed after just a week into the production run. The problem wasn't their design bottleneck, as Alice had thought it would be. All the slow downs and stops seemed to be in packaging.

"We've got twice the capacity we need in packaging to support this," she had previously calculated. But, this turned out not to be true in reality. It became apparent that packaging was their real, or operational, bottleneck, because of all the problems being experienced there.

Yes, Hardlee was right, more overtime, in fact more overtime than he really wanted.

"What?" Hardlee said, "I don't want to work late again tonight. I've been here late every night this week trying to get this damn packaging line to run right. My son's got a basketball game and I promised him I'd be there. I've got a life outside of work you know."

"I'm sorry, Hardlee, but you know how far behind we are on this launch," begged Allus.

"Oh yeah, the launch you were so proud of when we talked a month ago, when A&Z bought us. How do you feel now?" Hardlee sneered.

"Well you were looking forward to the overtime as I recall, Hardlee. What happened to all that enthusiasm for the extra money?" Allus responded, trying to maintain her cool.

"I'm tired of this crap," Hardlee shot back, " The damn thing stops or breaks down every hour, sometimes every few minutes, bags jam, drives trip, overflows cause us to have to stop it, photo cells cause trips when they're not supposed to, the labelers are a mess, we're throwing away more packages than we send to the warehouse, we seem to have enough time to fight the fires, but nobody is looking for the guy with the matches…." Hardlee droned on, hardly noticing that Allus had stopped listening and was rolling her eyes.

She finally held up her hands in a "surrender" sign as in "I give up". She had a military background.

"What?" Hardlee demanded, "You know I'm tellin' it like it is."

"Why don't we do something about this, and find the guy with the matches? Let's go talk to the plant engineer, P.E." Allus implored.

In a stroke of luck, P.E. happened to walk by right that instant, on his way to one end of the packaging line where yet another failure had occurred. He did not have a happy expression on his face. As Allus waved to him, he did a double take, almost as if he wanted to ignore her. He was a man on a mission.

"What?" he said impatiently.

"Could we talk for a minute?" implored Allus. She was doing a lot of imploring lately.

"I don't really have a minute," objected P.E.

"It's about this packaging line and all the problems we're having," Allus responded.

P.E. took a deep breath, "Yeah, my guys have been chasing their tails for a month on this damn thing. If it's not one problem, it's another. We're spending more time here than in any other part of the plant." Having vented a tiny bit, P.E. seemed a little calmer.

"The hurrier we go, the behinder we get," observed Hardlee, never one for subtlety, "Don't you think we oughta stop and take a deep breath and figure this out?"

P.E. stared at Hardlee intently, finally seeing the wisdom in his suggestion. "You're right," he finally said, after what seemed like a long time, but couldn't have been more than a few seconds, "I'll get back to you tomorrow morning."

After working with his guys to get the most recent problem resolved, P.E. called his old friend, Ben Friendly, and explained the situation.

Ben considered this briefly, and finally said, "I'm busy this week, but how 'bout we set something up for Monday afternoon. I'd like to meet with the people that run and maintain this line, an operating supervisor, a senior operator, a senior maintenance tech, the maintenance supervisor, and you. Let's say four hours, I want to really thrash out some of these issues."

P.E. hesitated, "Four hours?"

Ben replied dryly, "Hey, you're already behind over two weeks, and you'll be further behind on Monday. How much can four hours hurt, especially if we can resolve some of these issues? How much further behind are you going to get if we **don't** solve these problems?"

P.E. went to Alice Knervus to tell her about the planned meeting, Rod Stiff, the production manager, was in the office, apparently getting his butt chewed. As they say, doody flows downhill, and Rod was next in line for the doody.

"I've just had my butt chewed really good. If we can't get this resolved in the next week, and give the execs a good plan for moving forward, they're going to give this production run to another plant," Alice demanded, seeing her career taking a big hit if this happened.

Rod could only stare stiffly at Alice, and before he could respond, they both noticed Ben standing in the doorway. They turned to him with a collective "What?" It was none too friendly either.

"I have a proposal for getting the packaging line back on track to support production," P.E. said quickly, sensing the obvious tension in the room.

Alice and Rod seemed to calm down a bit, perhaps in desperation, though Rod couldn't resist taking a shot at P.E., "We would have nearly as many problems if you and your guys would just get off your butts and fix it right."

Alice jumped in quickly, "Rod, that was uncalled for. Let's all calm down."

"I'm sorry," Rod responded, "We're all under a lot of pressure."

P.E. let all that lay for a few seconds, and continued, "Well, first we need to sort out the nature of these problems. So, I need to convene a meeting on the packaging line with the operating supervisor, a senior operator, a senior maintenance tech, the maintenance supervisor,"

"Another meeting with my key guys, and your key guys, when we're already so far behind," exclaimed Rod, "We're never going to get back on track."

"Not until we sort the problems out," answered P.E., "Do you want to do that, or not?" There was a bit of sarcasm in the 'or not' part of the question.

Alice held up her hand as if to ask everyone to calm down, again, even though she was quite the Nervous Nellie inside. With a sense of desperation, she advised Rod and P.E. to have the meeting.

The following Monday, Ben Friendly arrived, and P.E. introduced him as someone who had looked at similar systems and helped other folks to solve problems like they were having. Everyone seemed a bit antsy.

Before everyone could get comfortable in a "meeting mode" Ben suggested the entire group go look at the packaging line, walking it down with them, asking about problems at each step of the packaging process, "What failures occur here? How often? What the consequence in terms of lost production?" This took more than two hours. Ben took copious notes.

Finally, they sat down for the meeting. Ben took the group through an analysis of the packaging line, first drawing a simple block diagram, and then for each step in the line, asking the same questions as he did on the floor, but engaging people in a discussion regarding the problems with the line. Concluding, he observed that they had considerable opportunity for improvement.

"Yeah, if that's what you want to call it," Hardlee said, just a hint sarcastically.

Then Ben proposed something that took everyone by surprise, "Tomorrow, I'd like to spend the entire day cleaning the packaging line."

He said this just as Rod Stiff walked in for the meeting. He hadn't joined them for the walk down, since he was more of a desk manager,

"What? We already clean the packaging line, and pretty regularly," protested Rod.

"Well, I want people to really clean it, make it sparkle, and incidentally, while they clean it, I want them to find the defects in the line, so they can correct them," responded Ben, in a friendly way. Continuing, he said, "We clean to inspect, as we inspect we detect problems, and then we correct those problems, so the line can run properly."

Rod was not particularly swayed by this argument, "We're already at less than half our production requirements and YOU want to CLEAN the line. What a bunch of crap."

Fortunately, after some arm twisting Ben had already cleared this approach with Alice that morning over breakfast. They had known each other previously at another site, where P.E. and Alice had worked together as well.

"Rod I appreciate the pressure you're under, but I've already cleared this with Alice."

"Fine, then Alice can take the heat if it doesn't work," Rod said stiffly.

The team spent the rest of the day getting ready to clean the packing line, collecting the appropriate cleaning materials and equipment. The next day, bright and early at 7am, they shut down the packaging line, isolated it, and began the cleaning process.

Ben admonished them before starting, "Remember what we discussed yesterday, and look for things that might be causing those problems." They found:

- The tare weight control was badly contaminated with product; and had not been calibrated in months.
- The bag magazine had bent loading racks- bags jammed; photo eyes and reflectors were misaligned.
- The cutters for the bag tops were different types and settings; and gummed up with lacquer from the bags – resulting in poor consistency of cuts.
- The glue pot was set 10 degrees too high, and the glue nozzles were fouled with dried glue.
- The mechanical "fingers" for spreading the bags were

bent; one had a bad sleeve bearing.

- Control cams were caked with grease, resulting in misalignment of bags, and jamming.
- Guides were bent and/or misaligned, and several bolts were loose or missing.
- Chains were loose, resulting in a jerking motion, and jamming, as the packaging progressed.
- Several bearings were worn out, or un-lubricated, or under-lubricated, or even over-lubricated.
- The palletizer had photo cells and reflectors misaligned or broken, un-calibrated limit switches, loose chains, and a faulty solenoid.
- The conveyor had poor tracking, poor "knockdown" bar settings, and poor shrink wrap settings.
- Lacquer from the bags had accumulated at major wear points resulting in jamming.

"Other than this, everything was in pretty good shape," Hardlee observed, "We were so busy cuttin' down the tree, we didn't take the time to sharpen our axe."

As they were working their way through all these issues, Alice Knervus appeared, seeming upset. "What's going on?" he asked.

"We're cleaning the packaging line, just like we discussed this morning," Ben advised.

"But you've been down for over four hours, and we've got product backed up," Alice countered.

"I didn't give you a specific timeline for this," Ben replied.

Alice was growing a little more irritated, "Damn it, a routine cleaning only takes a couple hours. How much longer is this going to take?"

"Probably the rest of the day," Ben said, "But before you get too upset, let me show you some things."

Ben took Alice from one end of the packaging line to the other, pointing out in fine detail all the defects the team had found.

At the end of the "tour", Ben said, "Until we get all these problems taken care of, you're going to get even further behind. What would you like me to do, *maam*? Adding emphasis to the word maam.

Alice heaved a long sigh, and replied in a none-too-friendly tone, and with a certain military bearing, "Carry on."

The team spent the rest of the day cleaning and correcting all these relatively minor problems, and before the next shift, the machine was humming, with output more than double what it had been.

Ben went to Alice's office, and stuck his head in the door. "What now?" Alice quizzed, still a little miffed.

"How 'bout coming out to the line with me?" Ben replied, smiling and friendly. They were soon there, and things were humming.

"With this production rate, you should get back on track in the next two or three weeks. We're running nearly triple what you've been running."

A broad smile crossed Alice's face. It was their bonding moment.

Following this, there were other actions that needed to be taken to assure that they sustained the improvements. These took place over the follow 6-18 months.

1. Developing a set of procedures and checklists for the packaging line to sustain the performance and avoid future defects, including the timing of all tasks needed.

2. Training and re-training all operators in the new procedures. For this, a digital camera was used to take pictures of each part of the line that went along with simple instructions for PM and setups. Each operator and supervisor had to "lay hands" on the packaging line to demonstrate they could do the tasks.

3. Changeovers were a major cause of lost production. So, standards and procedures were developed for changing each product, and operators trained in these standards.

4. There were big differences in practices between shifts for running the packaging line. Procedures were standardized and each shift participated in creating consistency of operation across all shifts.

5. Bag specifications and bag quality were a problem, creating a lot of jamming of the bags. Marketing had insisted on bag colors and quality, including triple lacquering to give the bags an eye-catching sheen, but that the supplier could not reliably meet. Steps were taken to work with the supplier to minimize this problem.

6. The hopper feeding the packaging machine was undersized for the duty required by the "launch", resulting in inconsistent feed rates. In a small capital project, the hopper was resized, eliminating this problem.

7. An Overall Equipment Effectiveness (OEE) measurement system was set up to allow the shifts to measure, and manage, all losses from ideal.

The Fido plant went on to achieve superior performance, and Alice was promoted to the next level.

The Lessons: 1) Take the time to sharpen your axe. It will make cutting the tree go a lot faster. 2) Once you have good practices in place, standardize those practices so that you sustain them.

The Mathberg Story

4

"What the hell?" fumed the maintenance manager, Abner Fumer, spewing out a litany of profanity better left for another kind of story, "How many times do we have to fix that damn thing? This is supposed to be a brand new plant."

The Mathberg plant, which was really a misnomer, since most of the people there were not particularly good at complex math, was starting up a new production process, and yet another failure had occurred. A better name for the new production plant might be iceberg. While it looked new and normal on the surface, there were just tons of problems lying beneath, and it was making progress at glacial speeds. This was the fourth shutdown this week that required emergency maintenance to get it going again. Starting a new plant or major production line was always a difficult effort, but this was ridiculous. Starting up the new Noki 1 production line had so far been the proverbial nightmare.

Fumer went quickly to the area of the plant where the problem was reported. There stood several people, Derf Nerdy, the area engineer, Ben Yerning, the production manager, and Gnavey Saylor, an ex-navy "nuc" technician, and the mechanic who was working on the machine, again.

"What the hell is it this time?" exclaimed Fumer, clearly exasperated. He'd been excoriated just the day before by Iman Ogre, the plant manager, about all the maintenance costs that were being incurred during startup and how Fumer's costs were running more than twice the budget.

Gnavey looked up, grease, dirt and oil covering much of his body, and plaintively said, "Bad design."

"Again?" Fumer boomed. "The problem yesterday was with the switches that weren't designed for the current load at startup. Well, we're not sure about this, since the spec on the switches indicated they should have been adequate, but they actually failed at startup because they had excess load. I did notice we got these from the Slopovian Republic, so who knows what the quality standards were. Guess we saved money on the project though," he finished, with a tone of defeated exasperation.

"The problem the day before on the pumps that were cavitating badly because of poor suction head," Fumer, continued to fume, though more quietly. "We had to re-run a twenty foot section of piping to get the suction right, and the access to the tanks was just awful. What should have been an eight hour job took 24 hours." All Derf Nerdy could do was nod in agreement.

All this time, Yerning was relatively quiet, but it was clear he was upset, "When are we going to get back on line?" he fussed with a low, almost hostile tone. He was far behind on the production ramp-up schedule and also had been "ripped a new one" the day before by Ogre. None of these guys had participated in the design process.

Meanwhile, back at headquarters, Acton Surly, was working on his next project, having passed the one-day (sometimes more like one-hour) acceptance tests on each subcomponent of Noki 1, and moving on. Surly was convinced that his new approach to projects, Minimum Adequate Design (MAD), was just the thing to assure a proper design within budget and on schedule. Indeed, he had demonstrated the success of this concept with the Noki 1 project, and was proud to explain it to anyone who asked, and even a few who didn't. "Noki 1 was on time and on budget," he proudly chirped.

These problems continued for the next 16 months, though they did diminish with time. After 18 months of effort in the startup phase, the plant finally achieved its design capability, but not without considerable expense, angst, and most importantly, loss of production output. During that period, the plant had been essentially sold out, and could have sold even more, had the plant been capable of delivering it.

A few weeks after the plant was finally running reasonably well, though still with a few problems, Bill Barnacal, VP of Operations, and a tenacious, stick-to-it kind of guy, decided to re-visit Noki 1 to determine what had been learned from this excruciatingly difficult project. He convened a meeting for that purpose. Unfortunately, Iman Ogre couldn't attend. He was on medical leave to recover from all the stress that had been induced in getting Noki 1 up and running. So, Barnacal invited Fumer, Yerning, and Surly. At this point, Acton Surly was defensive, having espoused the benefits of his MAD approach, but suffering from criticism from a number of directions, often behind his back. Fumer and Yerning were not on the best of terms at this point, given all the problems, some of which they tended to blame on each other, but they were coming to respect each other, given all the hardship both had suffered. But, they felt downright hostile toward Surly. So, the first meeting that Barnacal convened was a little tense.

Barnacal began the meeting with a simple question, "What did we learn from Noki 1?"

Fumer jumped in immediately, as if he was chomping at the bit to be heard, "We learned that Surly there doesn't know crap about how to design and install a plant."

Surly, of course, couldn't let that stand, and quickly shot back "Bullcrap, if you guys had just started the damn thing up like you were supposed to, we would have been online in three months instead of 18."

Barnacal raised his hands authoritatively, "All right that's enough. We're here to develop some new policies and practices, not to get into a big fight about who screwed up." He went on with a challenging tone, "I want everyone here to assume that everybody in this room wants to do a good job, and we're all working hard to do that. With that in mind, what have we learned, and what are we going to do differently? And, be civil to each other," he demanded.

Barnacal continued, "Surly, please describe your MAD process," which immediately brought muffled snickers. Barnacal gave Yerning and Fumer a stern look, at which point they both retreated. Surly proceeded to describe MAD, though a bit more timidly, and not nearly as confidently as he had in previous discussions. Surly was only beginning to understand the irony in his choice of the phrase minimum adequate design as a philosophy, and the results it had achieved so far.

Barnacal intoned, "All that sounds reasonable, reassuring Surly, but how did you determine minimum adequacy?" This question resulted in a long pregnant pause.

"Well, we have our specs for the equipment, various ASME, AIChE standards, along with statutory requirements, which define minimum requirements," Surly began, and then continued for a few minutes elaborating on these points, finishing with "and of course we have our budgets and schedules that are part of our minimum adequacy constraints. We also use work breakdown structure and critical path modeling to help us manage all this." It sounded reasonable.

"Did you ever talk with production or maintenance about your standards and how they would meet their requirements, about the problems and issues they might face with similar equipment and how you could address those in the design? What about startup, operability and maintainability issues, spare parts, and so on?" asked Barnacal, already having a good idea of what an accurate answer would be.

"Well, yes," Surly said somewhat defensively.

"Oh, bull crap," Fumer interrupted before Surly could say any more.

"Yeah, double bull," echoed Yerning, starting to sound childish.

"Remember what I just said," Barnacal said in low firm tone, then looking at Surly, "Go on."

Surly continued, "Well, we had two major design reviews that these guys or their representatives participated in. We had any number of small meetings on specific issues. We had a third design review planned, but these guys couldn't attend, so we cancelled it."

He started to continue, but Fumer and Yerning could hardly contain themselves. Barnacal motioned to them to speak.

Yerning went first for a change, "Yeah, you sent us a stack of drawings and spec sheets a mile thick the Thursday before the meeting and then demanded our input on Tuesday at the meeting. About all we could do was stumble through it. We should have had one of our senior people on your team, but you said it wasn't in your budget."

Fumer chimed in "Yeah, what he said."

Barnacal interjected, looking at Fumer "Why didn't you put someone from production and maintenance on the project out of your budget?"

"We didn't budget for any extra people in our maintenance budgets for that," responded Fumer, "you wouldn't let us."

"What he said," echoed Yerning.

"Oh," Barnacal thought out loud. He'd been under a lot of pressure on costs at the time.

Suddenly he felt a little embarrassed, but taking on his responsibility for the debacle that Noki 1 had become, Barnacal continued, "Let's spend a few minutes now talking about the problems we had in the construction, installation and startup phase, and more importantly, how we might avoid these or minimize them in the future...Ben."

Ben Yerning went into a litany of issues around startup, valves not being accessible for ease of isolation; control systems that had no spares for their PLC's; piping not long enough and tanks not located properly to minimize the risk of pump cavitation; pumps that were non-standard from those in the rest of the plant, and not particularly reliable; vessel entry locations that weren't accessible; drawings that said "run to suit".

At this point he sneered, "Run to suit, to suit who – us, or the contractor, or your budget?"

"Easy," Barnacal reminded him. "OK, let's hear from Fumer for a while."

Abner Fumer echoed many of the same problems with the equipment not being the same as that already on site, making it more difficult for his people to maintain it, and driving up the spares requirements, something he was under a lot of pressure to reduce. He described a litany of quality problems resulting in failures, poor access for maintenance, and all around poor design, at least poor from a maintainability standpoint.

Fumer was just getting warmed up, when Barnacal abruptly ended the discussion, "I think I've heard enough."

He continued, "In spite of all the difficulty with Noki 1, we've made enough money that the CEO, Harry Knuckles, has concluded that we need to expand our production capability again. Apparently he and the marketing guys continue to see a lot of growth for our products, and with good margins, in spite of what's happened with Noki 1, so he's asked me to explore building Noki 2. But, he was pretty adamant that he didn't want a repeat of Noki 1's problems."

"You're kidding," or perhaps words a little more salty, Fumer, Yerning and Surly said almost simultaneously. Eyes were wide in dis-belief; mouths were open in amazement.

"Close your mouths, for now," Barnacal said dryly.

"Yes, I was nearly as surprised as you," Barnacal responded to their wide eyes and open mouths, "I knew the products were being well received, and that in spite of our difficulty, we were making money, but didn't know we anticipated enough growth for another production line."

"In any event, here's what I'd like to do for Noki 2," Barnacal pulled up a graphic, and provided handouts which read:

1. We're going to have a senior operating supervisor and senior maintenance supervisor on the project team. That will be built into the project budget. And they can call in any of their staff they think are needed to get details of issues that need to be addressed.
2. We're going to have more, but smaller, project reviews, say one a month looking at subsystems. There will be one major review for the conceptual design, and one for the preliminary design.
3. The project engineers will be the maintenance engineers for their systems for two years after we complete startup. They will get the call at 2am on Saturday morning about equipment problems. I want these guys thinking longer term than just getting past the factory acceptance test.
4. There will be a process for charging back to the capital project any major errors found during the startup and for one year after we complete startup. This will be a form of warranty from the project. Likewise, I want the project manager to be thinking longer term than just the initial tests. I will be the arbitrator of these chargebacks. The project manager will include a warranty or chargeback allowance in his budget.
5. Spare parts will be built into the project budget. Fundamentally, for each equipment, we need to ask what fails most often, and make sure we have the parts necessary for that, particularly during startup. Insurance and critical spares will be taken on a case basis, each one considering the probability and consequence of failure compared to the carrying cost of capital.
6. Standard equipment will be used wherever possible. No cheap stuff from some unproven vendor is permitted. If you have a proposed exception, you have to run it by operations and maintenance managers, and

we have to account for any risk and do our research, including doing a pilot effort if appropriate.

7. Valves, pumps, fans, and so on will be located so as to make access for operation and maintenance easy. "Run to suit" on drawings is to be avoided.

"Your thoughts," he looked around at everyone.

Fumer and Yerning seemed pleased, but Surly was flexing his jaw muscles just a bit, and finally complained, "No. 3 and 4 look a bit onerous." He had never been held accountable for that.

Barnacal responded kindly, "We're not really negotiating here. I want you thinking longer term than just getting the project done, and moving on to your next project. I want you thinking more about the risk to the business if we don't do this one right."

Barnacal continued, "Even though we're not negotiating these principles, I do want your input and leadership so that these principles become a reality. Abner and Ben, I'd like you to draft up the requirements for no. 1 in each of your areas. Ben, you draft up something for no. 2. Acton, you handle no. 3 and 4. Abner, you handle no. 5 and 6, and Ben, you handle no. 7. We'll review each other's proposals, let's say one a week. I'll have my administrative assistant organize the sessions. If you have any other suggestions that you think would help us do this right, feel free to add those."

He continued, "I'm expecting we'll begin on the conceptual design sometime in this quarter, so we should have enough time to get some of these requirements hammered out before then."

Some six months later they received the approval to proceed with Noki 2. At this point, Iman Ogre had returned and was a bit bum-fuzzled at all the changes that had taken place in projects, but with all his therapy was much more mellow and receptive to them.

Staff from Noki 1 were involved deeply in the specification and design phases, since they knew most of the issues and problems in the original design. Budgets were provided for this participation, and the project manager was finally very supportive of all this. He had finally come around to Barnacal's position, and since he had been the project manager for Noki 1, he was determined to do a better job on Noki 2, without being MAD.

The results were remarkable. Noki 2 was brought to full production in just three months, and has been consistently more reliable and less costly than Noki 1. Perhaps as importantly, the cost of Noki 2 was not significantly different from Noki 1, but the performance, both at startup and during normal operation was remarkably better. They had saved enough in the construction phase, by eliminating most of the re-work that would have otherwise occurred, to pay for the extra cost of the design effort. An even more important result of applying life cycle principles in the design of Noki 2 was the impact of its success on the plant's culture. Fumer, Yerning and Surly actually became friends and enjoyed working together. By doing the right things and witnessing success with their own eyes, they and their people started believing in systems and processes. They worked together toward a common purpose, rather than relying on gut feel, last year's memories, and focusing on their little kingdom. This greatly assisted in driving further improvement and equip them to better to face the future challenges - no one wants to go back to the trial and error days of Noki 1! The business is currently prospering with record profits.

The Lesson: 1) If you only focus on your project and only on getting it done, you may do in the business. 2) Applying life cycle cost principles works better than lowest installed cost principles. 3) Using a MAD philosophy can be maddening.

A Tale of Two Plants

5

They were the best of plants, and the worst of plants, these two.

They were part of the same company. They were both the same vintage, so the big differences between them couldn't be due to age. They both had similar technology, so it couldn't be the technology. They both had similar business models, so it didn't seem to be strategy. They both had similar organizational structures, so it probably wasn't that. They were both unionized, and indeed both unions were somewhat "militant", and relationships with management could certainly be better, so it's not that either. They both had similar energy and raw material costs, so that's not it either.

How could such two such extremes exist in the same company? Why the difference between these two plants?

Going back about five years ago, we could see the situation in the business and at both operations. Costs were increasing and prices falling, and the business was under considerable pressure to improve production, productivity, and lower costs.

At the Workinhard plant, the plant manager, Ian Nutaprittie, wasn't very articulate, and didn't have a strong so-called "presence" in a meeting. At times he would mumble, sometimes to himself. He just didn't leave a good first impression. He wasn't getting high marks from senior management, mostly because of this.

That said, he had the respect of all his people. They knew they could depend on him to do what he said, that he was fair and honest, and that he rarely challenged people to do more than was reasonable. With costs increasing and prices falling, Ian was under considerable pressure to improve production, and lower costs. So, he decided to initiate an improvement program, using a multi-phased approach to improve performance.

Ian made it clear that getting better was not an option, it was a requirement. He focused intensely on defect elimination, using cross-functional teams and getting the processes right. Costs were viewed as consequences of the processes. He reasoned that if you get them right, you'll get better results. While there were other initiatives being imposed on the plant, he acted as a filter relative to their priority. His reasoning was that if they got the basics right in the first place, then the other initiatives would be easier to implement. The process basically involved the following:

> Phase 1: Alignment of the leadership and area teams to focus on doing all the basics really well to minimize defects and failures.
> Phase 2: Benchmarking, identifying the gaps and developing a plan to close the gaps over a 24 month period. The plan included the systems to sustain the improvements.
> Phase 3: Implementing the action plan using a coach-team model with the ownership of the processes remaining with the team in each area.
> Phase 4: Sustaining the results – developing and implementing procedures, checklists, standards, and a continuous improvement process, modeled after the proverbial Plan, Do, Check, Act that Deming suggested decades ago, to constantly look for ways to make them even better.

Meanwhile at the Buena Vista plant, the plant manager, I.B. Lukengud, which was in a similar situation, they too were working hard to improve. Unfortunately, IB, as he preferred to be called, sent two conflicting messages- 1) Cut costs; 2) Improve practices. But, he placed much more emphasis on cost cutting. These messages were exacerbated by the same multiple initiatives. IB was being driven intensely to cut costs, and he was apparently unable to appropriately filter and prioritize all the initiatives. This in turn diluted the focus of the organization, and its potential for success.

For example, one directive was to reduce labor costs by 2% and overall costs by 5% in the coming year. Yet the improvement effort had just begun, and the plant was relatively immature in its practices. Any improvement effort, particularly in an immature plant, will require some investment, notwithstanding that it often achieves a "pay as you go" result after 6-12 months. If short-term resources aren't available to implement the improvements needed because of cost cutting, the plant can put its future success at risk.

Initially the cost cutting approach at Buena Vista seemed to be working, and indeed "kudos"were given to IB in the first two years. However, the various practices that should have been established to sustain the performance were not done. As a result in the third year and later, production performance suffered, making the cost per unit substantially higher. That's the illusion in using a cost cutting strategy in most cases – initially it seems to be working, but is typically not sustainable. Unfortunately, it's common that the manager who made the decision to do the cost cutting in the first two to three years is no longer there when the results begin to deteriorate, primarily because of a lack of sustainability, and thus that manager will suffer no ill effect from his or her decisions.

Two nearly identical plants achieved nearly opposite results. Why? In one scenario, the plant manager focused on defect elimination, getting the processes right, and engaging the workforce using cross-functional teams. He made it clear that improvement and cost reduction were mandatory. He also made it clear that the focus was getting the processes right, and sustaining them; and he acted as a filter for prioritizing corporate initiatives.

In the second scenario, the plant manager focused on cost cutting, and in the first two years saw some improvement, only to see those improvements disappear and the situation become even worse in subsequent years. He did not do a very good job of filtering and prioritizing the initiatives, attempting to be all things to all people.

Which approach would you take?

The Lesson: A focus on cost cutting will not provide sustainable results. Costs are a consequence of your processes. Get your processes right, engaging your people in helping you create those processes, and the right things will happen.

Part IV

Being Rich

Being Rich –
A Question of Perspective

I'd like to close the book with a personal story. It's a kind of parable, but quite true.

I was doing a manufacturing practices workshop in England many years ago, and while covering the section regarding compensation, one of the attendees remarked "Easy for you to say, you're rich." I don't remember the exact part of the discussion prompted him to make this comment. Perhaps it was my comment that money is generally not a motivator. He did, however, catch me off guard. I stood a bit flummoxed for a moment and then said:

> "You know, you're right, I'm rich. I've got a wife that loves me, and I love dearly. We enjoy each other's company. I've got six kids and several grandkids that I love dearly and get along with really well. I've got great parents, and so does my wife, and all of us get along really well. I've got good friends. I'm healthy. I really enjoy my work. You're right, I'm rich."

He had no response, so we carried on with the workshop.

Growing up in the tiny hamlet of Garrett in eastern Kentucky in the 50's, we had little money. Dad had just returned from the WWII, where he was a genuine hero landing on the beaches of Leyte and Okinawa, having been decorated twice for bravery and wounded in action, receiving the Purple Heart. After the war, the only job available to him locally was working as a coal miner in small mines that paid very little, and has no benefits.

Mom worked as a clerk at her Dad's small country store after we started school. We lived the proverbial "hand-to-mouth" day–to-day existence. I never felt poor. We always had plenty to eat (we had our own vegetable garden in the summer) and a warm house (well, there was a layer of ice on the windows during the coldest days of winter), clean clothes, and above all, unconditional love.

The local elementary school was a small four-room schoolhouse with no indoor plumbing, a potbelly coal-fired stove in the middle of each room to keep us warm, and two grades per room. The high school wasn't much bigger, though it did have indoor plumbing and central heating, but no air conditioning. We only had 42 in my graduating class. I didn't know it then, but in retrospect, most of my teachers were excellent. I went on to West Point, and ultimately earned a bachelor's degree in engineering, a master's in engineering, and a master's in business. This was all made possible because I had excellent teachers in elementary and high school, who were demanding and set high expectations, but simultaneously very caring – Mr. Case, Mrs. Prater, Mr. Martin, and Mrs. Fouts were particularly good.

I loved and enjoyed my grandparents, and continue to have many, many fond memories of them. Most memories around Mamaw Moore relate to food, around Papaw Moore to his kind nature. Most around Papaw Scott relate to his kindness as well and his business acumen running his small country store. I never knew Mamaw Scott – she died in childbirth before I was born, but my step-grandma was always good to me. We lived a Walton-like life. Most people today would call us disadvantaged, or poor. We had little money, but we were rich in all the things that you wouldn't take money for – great family, good health, great teachers, great friends, and lots of love.

Today, I'm still rich in these things, and I'm far wealthier financially than I ever imagined growing up. Unfortunately, my riches are dwindling. My father has passed away, along with my wife's father, both in the same year. My wife's mother has also passed away. My mother is in the sunset of her life as well. We're both so grateful to have had them as long as we did, and cherish the memories. All their deaths were a tremendous loss in our riches.

We still have good health, even though my wife has had a brain tumor removed, and a liver transplant, which have left her with less than ideal health. But, we're rich – she's alive and doing well in spite of the few impediments from the surgeries, and we continue to enjoy each other's company. Our riches are even greater in some respects, with the addition of several grandkids, such that we now have 14. I still enjoy my work, and remain healthy (knock on wood as they say).

Now that I have enough money that I don't worry about next month's paycheck, it's easier to appreciate what we had then, and have now. Yes, money is important, and you need enough money to take care of day-to-day living. But, you might want to count your riches in other ways.

The Lesson: To determine how rich you are, ask yourself – "What do I have that I wouldn't trade for money?" Too many people seek riches that make them poor.

About the Author

Ron Moore lives with his wife Kathy in Knoxville, TN, where they are employees of The RM Group, Inc., a manufacturing management consulting firm. They were high school, then college sweethearts, but parted ways. To make a long story short, they came together again some 20 years later, and now have between them six children, 15 grandchildren (sadly, one deceased), and one great grandchild. Ron has a BS and MS in mechanical engineering, along with a MBA, while Kathy has a BA in art. Their very different perspectives, combined with their very similar values, provide balance in their relationship, and ultimately make for a very kind and loving life together.

CPSIA information can be obtained at www.ICGtesting.com
Printed in the USA
BVOW022209230613

324079BV00006BA/38/P